I0015462

KnockoutJS Web Development

Efficiently work with data, web templates, and custom
HTML tags using KnockoutJS

John Farrar

PUBLISHING

BIRMINGHAM - MUMBAI

KnockoutJS Web Development

Copyright © 2015 Packt Publishing

All rights reserved. No part of this book may be reproduced, stored in a retrieval system, or transmitted in any form or by any means, without the prior written permission of the publisher, except in the case of brief quotations embedded in critical articles or reviews.

Every effort has been made in the preparation of this book to ensure the accuracy of the information presented. However, the information contained in this book is sold without warranty, either express or implied. Neither the author, nor Packt Publishing, and its dealers and distributors will be held liable for any damages caused or alleged to be caused directly or indirectly by this book.

Packt Publishing has endeavored to provide trademark information about all of the companies and products mentioned in this book by the appropriate use of capitals. However, Packt Publishing cannot guarantee the accuracy of this information.

First published: February 2015

Production reference: 1210215

Published by Packt Publishing Ltd.
Livery Place
35 Livery Street
Birmingham B3 2PB, UK.

ISBN 978-1-78216-102-8

www.packtpub.com

Credits

Author
John Farrar

Reviewers
Paul Manzotti

Julia Rechkunova

Tatsuro Shibamura

Cristian Trifan

Saul Wiggin

Commissioning Editor
Mary Nadar

Acquisition Editor
Nikhil Karkal

Content Development Editor
Manasi Pandire

Technical Editor
Prajakta Mhatre

Copy Editors
Puja Lalwani

Vikrant Phadke

Laxmi Subramanian

Project Coordinator
Leena Purkait

Proofreaders
Simran Bhogal

Maria Gould

Paul Hindle

Chris Smith

Indexer
Mariammal Chettiyar

Production Coordinator
Manu Joseph

Cover Work
Manu Joseph

About the Author

John Farrar is a man who has a passion for pragmatic technology. He started working on computers in the late 70s and has watched the trends as closely as he watches the milestones. His work included programming on early computers, repairing military flight simulators in the navy, and working on web technology that helps people get business done. This work included building early commerce solutions for Apple, Brunswick Recreation, and Casio and working for a number of other companies along the letters of the alphabet. He is inspired and passionate about understanding the need before choosing the technology that answers the challenge.

Over the years, John has worked on a couple of books for ColdFusion, multiple open source projects from early Fusebox, community participation with jQuery, and some frameworks he created on his own. He has spoken at about a dozen conferences over the years and worked on supporting local and online users as time has permitted. He has provided technical training from online courses, in person class instructions, and a number of great intern programmers that let him share their entrance into the world of writing software.

I believe no man rises on his own strength and I appreciate the incredible number of friends in the community who give and share time and technology. Every place I have worked and every community that I spent time at has enriched and challenged me. Without you, my technology and understanding would be a fraction of what it is. Thanks for being part of my journey.

About the Reviewers

Paul Manzotti created his first website in 1995, running the newly released CERN httpd on a spare Silicon Graphics machine in the lab he was working in.

A decade of designing websites progressing into mild programming using Microsoft's ASP technology ended with him going back to university to gain an MSc in computer programming.

Then he came out fully armed as a programmer and started using ASP.NET with a lot of heavy JavaScript work; that's what single-page applications (SPA) are all about. And hence, when single-page applications became a thing, he was more than happy to dive into it.

He is a senior developer at Purple Bricks (https://www.purplebricks.com/).

Julia Rechkunova is a software engineer who is inspired by web development and design. She has over 4 years of experience and focuses on the quality and usability of web applications. She enjoys working as a frontend developer as well as a backend developer. Modern web technologies and tools are the best instruments that help her build great applications and make the world better. She graduated with a master's degree in computer science, started working as an HTML5 game developer, and then participated in start ups. She has a passion for frontend programming and contributes to open source projects. Currently, she works with technologies such as HTML5, CSS3, JavaScript, Node.js, and other popular frameworks. Julia also likes creating new tools that bring something different to the industry.

Tatsuro Shibamura is a Microsoft MVP of ASP.NET/IIS. He develops applications that use the Azure websites and ASP.NET MVC architecture in Japan. He has mainly used Knockout.js as a client-side technology. Thanks to that, it has received the advice to Akira Inoue's Microsoft Japan.

Cristian Trifan is a full-time developer based in Cluj-Napoca, Romania. He started developing ERP desktop applications in .NET about 10 years ago but switched to web development as he felt more attracted to Node.js and single page applications. As a pragmatic perfectionist, he's constantly seeking to improve himself. Apart from his job, he's also a contributor to the Knockout-Validation library.

He is currently working at Acunetix, building the frontend for their Online Vulnerability Scanner. It is a single page application that provides security scanning services to users who need to protect their web applications and perimeter networks. Its strong focus is on simplicity and usability while maintaining a high level of security in the system.

Saul Wiggin completed a PhD in transformation optics and metamaterials from the Department for Electronic Engineering and Computer Science at Queen Mary University of London. His thesis was on applications for transformation optics to engineering electromagnetic waves and optics. He worked with the QUEST platform grant. He presented his research at international conferences: META12 in Paris and EUCAP 2014 in Orlando Florida. His square Luneberg Lens was patented by BAE systems. Prior to this, he completed his master's at the University of Manchester in physics, where his final year project involved astrophysical simulations of Masers around late-type stars using Fortran and IDL, and he discovered evidence for the existence of a radio photosphere near to the stellar surface. His supervisors were Professor Clive Parini FRS, Professor Ian Youngs (DSTL), and Dr. Malcom Grey at the centre for astrophysics at the University of Manchester. He was funded partly by the EPRSC and partly by DSTL. He has written books on parallel programming in Haskell and worked on the open source project Ropensci, which led to a package being distributed on cran.

www.PacktPub.com

Support files, eBooks, discount offers, and more

For support files and downloads related to your book, please visit www.PacktPub.com.

Did you know that Packt offers eBook versions of every book published, with PDF and ePub files available? You can upgrade to the eBook version at www.PacktPub.com and as a print book customer, you are entitled to a discount on the eBook copy. Get in touch with us at service@packtpub.com for more details.

At www.PacktPub.com, you can also read a collection of free technical articles, sign up for a range of free newsletters and receive exclusive discounts and offers on Packt books and eBooks.

https://www2.packtpub.com/books/subscription/packtlib

Do you need instant solutions to your IT questions? PacktLib is Packt's online digital book library. Here, you can search, access, and read Packt's entire library of books.

Why subscribe?
- Fully searchable across every book published by Packt
- Copy and paste, print, and bookmark content
- On demand and accessible via a web browser

Free access for Packt account holders

If you have an account with Packt at www.PacktPub.com, you can use this to access PacktLib today and view 9 entirely free books. Simply use your login credentials for immediate access.

Table of Contents

Preface	**1**
Chapter 1: Getting Started with KnockoutJS	**5**
Installing KnockoutJS	**5**
Looking at MVVM	**6**
Binding DOM elements using Knockout	**7**
Binding text	8
Binding HTML	9
Binding CSS	10
Binding numbers	10
Managing visibility	11
Multibound control	12
Power development using browser developer tools	**13**
The Knockout debugger	15
Shortcuts	16
The DOM inspection	17
The AJAX inspection	17
The resource inspection	17
The device emulation	17
Using internal functions with Knockout	**18**
Preventing hidden features	20
Automating calculations with Knockout	**20**
Subtotal calculation	22
Tax time	23
Final total	25
Working with non-Knockout functions	**26**
Summary	**27**

Chapter 2: Using Arrays, Nesting, and Grids	**29**
Conditional binding	**29**
Introduction to arrays in Knockout	**31**
Working with array collections	33
Removing the last item	37
Sorting time	**38**
The simpleGrid plugin	**41**
Running the code	42
Final sort	47
Summary	**49**
Chapter 3: Giving Forms the Knockout Touch	**51**
Event binding	**51**
The binding markup	52
The binding checkbox with visibility	54
Modifier keys	55
Default actions	56
Preventing bubbling	57
The textInput binding	**57**
Dynamic focus	58
Radio and checkbox binding	**62**
Enhanced event integration	65
Select binding	**66**
Selecting elements with the object collections	68
Listing the management Knockout style	70
The uniqueName binding	**72**
Grid forms	**72**
Summary	**75**
Chapter 4: Coding – AJAX, Binding Properties, Mapping, and Utilities	**77**
JSON done Knockout style	**78**
Mapping – first look	**81**
Connecting with AJAX remotely	**82**
Unmapping your data	**85**
Merging mapped data	**87**
Mapping options	**88**
Utility functions	**88**
ko.utils.arrayFilter()	88
ko.utils.arrayFirst()	90
ko.utils.arrayMap()	91
ko.utils.arrayGetDistinctValues ()	92

ko.utils.arrayForEach()	93
ko.utils.compareArrays()	94
Purifying our computations	**95**
Coding documents for computed observables	**97**
Form 1	97
Form 2	98
Form 3	98
Form 4	99
Using a computed observable	**99**
Using the computed context	**99**
Summary	**100**
Chapter 5: The Joy of Templates	**101**
Native templates	**101**
Enhanced collection handling	**107**
Render event handling	**112**
Third-party template options	**114**
Modified template handling with Underscore	116
Live updates and the subscribe method in Knockout	117
Awesome template options	**121**
Summary	**124**
Chapter 6: Packaged Elegance	**127**
Introduction to components	**127**
Dynamic component selection	130
Bring Your Own Tags (BYOT)	131
Enhancing attribute handling	**131**
Building your own libraries	**133**
Bootstrap component example	136
Understanding the AMD approach	**138**
Component-based SPAs	**141**
Best development strategies	142
Getting real	142
Coding time	144
Adding navigation	147
Adding pages	148
Time for some custom style	149
Bonus item	154
Building cross-page interaction	154
What next?	**157**
Summary	**157**
Index	**159**

Preface

Good tools make the Internet responsive and interactive and put its control in the hands of developers. The Knockout library is well-known because it is a pair of boxing gloves that work well in the ring! What jQuery did for JavaScript years ago, Knockout is doing for smart data management with the browser elements. With this library, you will find another way to enjoy building web technology, while building sites that end users will enjoy just as much. If you know the basics of JavaScript and HTML, this book will soon make you a champion.

What this book covers

Chapter 1, Getting Started with KnockoutJS, teaches you what Knockout is and why it is different. This chapter gets you coding and opens the door to a simpler and more powerful way of building web pages.

Chapter 2, Using Arrays, Nesting, and Grids, continues opening your mind to less code with more power. There is special coverage on dynamic sorting of data collections that will put power coding in the hands of newer developers.

Chapter 3, Giving Forms the Knockout Touch, demonstrates the use of Knockout to make our web forms easier and fun to build. This covers both simple and grid-based forms.

Chapter 4, Coding – AJAX, Binding Properties, Mapping, and Utilities, proves that Knockout is not just a stand-alone solution. It is a technology that connects and simplifies our interaction, and it has a number of awesome plugins that will make you eager to use it in your projects.

Chapter 5, The Joy of Templates, covers native templates, enhanced collection handling, render events, third-party templates, and a few more template options.

Chapter 6, *Packaged Elegance*, takes you into the future of web development. This chapter covers present-day use of custom components in all popular browsers. We will use this opportunity to cover another way of building a simplified and powerful SPA, single-page applications, and solutions.

What you need for this book

First, you will need a computer with a web server. The examples will run on any common server, so a special server-side language is not required. You will need a text editor, and if you want to use the exercise files, you will need to be able to decompress a ZIP file. There is a built-in provision for this in most modern computers. Finally, you will need a browser to view your work.

Who this book is for

This book is for web developers or web designers who work with HTML and wants to gain knowledge while making things simple. This will show you how to automate, with some simple markup, the interaction between your data and the visual side of the browser. If you are looking to get the best experience with cleaner and more sustainable code, this book will serve you well.

Conventions

In this book, you will find a number of text styles that distinguish between different kinds of information. Here are some examples of these styles and explanations of their meanings.

Code words in text, database table names, folder names, filenames, file extensions, pathnames, dummy URLs, user input, and Twitter handles are shown as follows: "We will need to use the `push` method of our bound array collection to add this."

A block of code is set as follows:

```
<button data-bind="click: sort('name')">Sort By Name</button>
<button data-bind="click: sort('item')">Sort By Item</button>
```

When we wish to draw your attention to a particular part of a code block, the relevant lines or items are set in bold:

```
this.orderVM = new ko.simpleGrid.viewModel({
data: this.orders,
columns: [
```

```
   { headerText: "Customer", rowText: "name"},
   { headerText: "Item", rowText: "item"},
   { headerText: "Count", rowText: "qty"}
   ],
   pageSize: 3
   });
```

Any command-line input or output is written as follows:

```
> pagedOrderModel.orders()
```

New terms and **important words** are shown in bold. Words that you see on the screen, for example, in menus or dialog boxes, appear in the text like this: "Click on the **Add Staff** button."

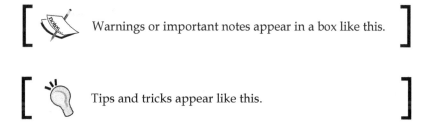

Warnings or important notes appear in a box like this.

Tips and tricks appear like this.

Reader feedback

Feedback from our readers is always welcome. Let us know what you think about this book—what you liked or disliked. Reader feedback is important for us as it helps us develop titles that you will really get the most out of.

To send us general feedback, simply e-mail feedback@packtpub.com, and mention the book's title in the subject of your message.

If there is a topic that you have expertise in and you are interested in either writing or contributing to a book, see our author guide at www.packtpub.com/authors.

Customer support

Now that you are the proud owner of a Packt book, we have a number of things to help you to get the most from your purchase.

Downloading the example code

You can download the example code files from your account at http://www.packtpub.com for all the Packt Publishing books you have purchased. If you purchased this book elsewhere, you can visit http://www.packtpub.com/support and register to have the files e-mailed directly to you.

Errata

Although we have taken every care to ensure the accuracy of our content, mistakes do happen. If you find a mistake in one of our books—maybe a mistake in the text or the code—we would be grateful if you could report this to us. By doing so, you can save other readers from frustration and help us improve subsequent versions of this book. If you find any errata, please report them by visiting http://www.packtpub.com/submit-errata, selecting your book, clicking on the **Errata Submission Form** link, and entering the details of your errata. Once your errata are verified, your submission will be accepted and the errata will be uploaded to our website or added to any list of existing errata under the Errata section of that title.

To view the previously submitted errata, go to https://www.packtpub.com/books/content/support and enter the name of the book in the search field. The required information will appear under the **Errata** section.

Piracy

Piracy of copyrighted material on the Internet is an ongoing problem across all media. At Packt, we take the protection of our copyright and licenses very seriously. If you come across any illegal copies of our works in any form on the Internet, please provide us with the location address or website name immediately so that we can pursue a remedy.

Please contact us at copyright@packtpub.com with a link to the suspected pirated material.

We appreciate your help in protecting our authors and our ability to bring you valuable content.

Questions

If you have a problem with any aspect of this book, you can contact us at questions@packtpub.com, and we will do our best to address the problem.

1
Getting Started with KnockoutJS

Welcome to the power and wonder of the world of KnockoutJS. In this chapter, we will start down the road to win with AJAX HTML applications AJAX HTML applications. This chapter will focus on:

- Installing KnockoutJS
- Understanding what MVVM means
- Binding elements with the Knockout library
- Accelerating and simplifying coding using developer tools in modern browsers
- Creating functions for consumption with Knockout
- Automating the computing of values directly with Knockout
- Working with functions outside of Knockout

Installing KnockoutJS

First, make sure you have a working website set up on a server. It can be as simple as plain old HTML if you only want to learn those features or any of the productive web platforms out there (ASP.NET, ColdFusion/Railo, NodeJS, PHP, Python, Ruby, and so on); just make sure the service is running before installing Knockout. However, there is one exception. If you are using Knockout for an HTML application like PhoneGap or something along those lines, then you do not need a web server for internal functionality.

There are a number of ways to install Knockout. You need to choose the one that works right for you. The book files have been packaged into a ZIP file at `http://knockout.developers.zone/books/knockout-js-web-development/`. Click on the link to download the current stable release of the product. We will keep it up to date with fixes if any are needed. We will also be creating a video on that page to show how to get things installed at least on Mac and Windows.

If you download the page directly from the Knockout site at `http://knockoutjs.com`, copy the text and paste it into a JS file within the folders for your website.

Now, there are others who may be using fancier tools in the future. There are several package installers that pull the files needed. If you are using one of those for this book then check that the version of KnockoutJS is 3.2 or later. I would suggest not using those at this time unless you are already familiar with them. They are worth getting to know but not needed to get running with Knockout.

My examples include the Bootstrap library as I wanted to improve the presentation and give a distinct personality on the pages of this book, which is another way of saying it made creating this resource for you more fun for me.

I have links to all the examples and exercises in this book linked from the root of the web folder. I would suggest learning to use Knockout there, and using this knowledge if you are moving to web-based app development.

With the files loaded, you should be able to click through a couple of the examples. One of my goals was to set the course up so you could use this as a quick reference document after completing the course when you need to look up how to do different things with Knockout.

Your work pages should go in the appropriate folder matching the chapter numbers of this book. I have created complete working examples in the done folder and yours should go into the do folder under the matching chapter number.

Looking at MVVM

MVVM is a design approach to building software. The name is a little confusing, and it makes you wonder if they were trying to be clear or if they just liked the symmetry that the letters created. The design pattern was used extensively in Microsoft and Apple development products.

MVVM stands for **Model View ViewModel**.

Let's start with the **View**. It is where the HTML is converted to **Document Object Model (DOM)**.

The View interacts with an object called a ViewModel. The **ViewModel** is where the presentation logic is stored. The **Model** is the part that stores the data and business logic. This is commonly passed to the browser as a JSON object.

Let's clear up a confusing point right now. When charted out, most people draw out the relationship as View-ViewModel-Model, which would be VVMM. Don't get caught up in the semantics; just take a look at the following diagram to understand what they mean by MVVM:

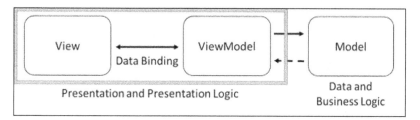

Your data gets stored in the Model, but you do not interact with the data directly. You use the ViewModel to interact with the data. You should also note that you don't need to be an expert with the MVVM pattern, as the concepts in practice are very simple. The evidence of this is the simplicity of binding elements to the ViewModel.

Binding DOM elements using Knockout

There are two basic ways to bind your View elements to the ViewModel. You can either bind it through the element `data-bind` attribute or by using friendly code in JavaScript. Let's begin by creating a page in the `\ko\ko-1\do\` folder using the name `binding.htm`. The following is the basic standard code for your `do` pages throughout the book:

```
<!DOCTYPE html>
<html lang="en">
<head>
</head>
<body>
<script src="/share/js/knockout.js"></script>
<script type="text/javascript">
var viewModel = {
}
ko.applyBindings(viewModel);
</script>
</body>
</html>
```

Downloading the example code

You can download the example code files from your account at
http://www.packtpub.com for all the Packt Publishing books
you have purchased. If you purchased this book elsewhere, you
can visit http://www.packtpub.com/support and register
to have the files e-mailed directly to you.

The first part of using Knockout is to include the library JS file. Then we need to
create the ViewModel. At this time, the ViewModel is similar to a class file as it
does not do anything until we bind it using Knockout's `applyBindings` method.
The name of the Model does not matter to Knockout as long, of course, as it does
not conflict with JS or some other currently running library.

Binding text

To bind the text to the ViewModel, use the following steps:

1. Add the following code to the ViewModel:

```
var viewModel = {
  myVariable: ko.observable()}
```

2. We will use the `data-bind` attribute to tell Knockout how to bind our data
   through the ViewModel. We bind the text attribute of this DOM element to
   the ViewModel variable `myVariable`. After the `body` tag, add this code:

```
My first KnockoutJS uses text binding: <span data-bind="text:
myVariable"></span>
<hr>
```

3. We are now ready to run the code. When you look at the code in the browser
   nothing appears to happen. That is because there is no value assigned to the
   ViewModel variable, so nothing gets injected into the View. It gives us the
   following text in the browser window:

   My first KnockoutJS uses text binding

4. Let's add one more line below the line where we bind the ViewModel in
   our script:

```
ko.applyBindings(viewModel);
viewModel.myVariable("Awesome simple!");
```

The code gives us a value to be assigned, and when we run the page it shows the data bound to the DOM element. The following text is the output in the browser window:

My first KnockoutJS uses text binding: Awesome simple!

Here, we see that the text attribute of the HTML DOM element updated when the variable was updated. There was no need to directly update the HTML DOM element as the ViewModel feature of Knockout automates this feature. In large and complex data sets, Knockout has been tested as the fastest data bound library. Of course, this consideration might change over time.

Binding HTML

To bind HTML to the ViewModel use the following steps:

1. Add the HTML code to the ViewModel:

```
var viewModel = {
  myVariable: ko.observable(),
  myHTML: ko.observable()
}
```

2. Set the value of the myHTML variable after the binding of the ViewModel:

```
viewModel.myVariable("Awesome simple!");
viewModel.myHTML("<strong>Awesome</strong> simple!");
```

3. Now, we need to bind the HTML attribute of the DOM element. As you can see, the syntax is very similar to the text binding we used in the last binding:

```
My second KO uses HTML binding:
<div data-bind="html: myHTML"></div>
<hr>
```

If we pass HTML through to the text element, it does not display correctly, and that is why DOM has a particular HTML attribute for appropriate tags. When we use the text approach, Knockout escapes the results and using HTML, places the results the way it would look in an editor. The HTML attribute does not exist every time the text attribute exists, but it is pretty safe to assume that the text does exist any time we find the HTML at this point. When we render again, Knockout renders the text as shown here:

My second KO uses HTML binding:
Awesome simple!

Binding CSS

To bind CSS to the ViewModel go through the following steps:

1. Add the myLeft and myRight variables to the ViewModel:

    ```
    var viewModel = {
      myVariable: ko.observable()
      ,myHTML: ko.observable()
      ,myLeft: ko.observable()
      ,myRight: ko.observable()
    }
    ```

2. Set the values of the `myLeft` and `myRight` variables after the binding of the ViewModel:

    ```
    viewModel.myVariable("Awesome simple!");
    viewModel.myHTML("<strong>Awesome</strong> simple!");
    viewModel.myLeft("pullLeft");
    viewModel.myRight("pushRight");
    ```

3. Use the CSS attribute to the `data-bind` setting to manage CSS dynamically through the ViewModel. This could be changed at any time, and the elements would reflect the CSS settings based on how, of course, the individual browser responds to those CSS settings.

    ```
    <div data-bind="css: myLeft">LEFT </div>
    <div data-bind="css: myRight"> RIGHT</div>
    My third KO uses CSS binding:
    <hr>
    ```

When we render again, Knockout renders the text as shown here:

```
LEFT My third KO uses CSS binding:                              RIGHT
```

Binding numbers

The following steps will explain how to bind numbers to the ViewModel:

1. Add the following code to the ViewModel:

    ```
    var viewModel = {
      myVariable: ko.observable()
      ,myHTML: ko.observable()
      ,myLeft: ko.observable()
      ,myRight: ko.observable()
    ```

```
    ,myBalance: ko.observable()
}
```

2. Set the value of the `myBalance` variable after the binding of the ViewModel:

```
viewModel.myVariable("Awesome simple!");
viewModel.myHTML("<strong>Awesome</strong> simple!");
viewModel.myLeft("pullLeft");
viewModel.myRight("pushRight");
viewModel.myBalance(-47.23);
```

Here, we explore our first `data-bind` where we are binding to more than one setting at the same time via the HTML markup. Notice that we also wrapped the element with an additional outer element to allow us to set the color for the balance based on whether it is negative or not. When we are doing this, we can insert a bit of JavaScript into the setting. When using JavaScript, we refer to `myBalance` as a function and not as a variable because that is how we interact with it in JavaScript. Take a look at the following code:

```
My fourth KO uses Style binding:<br>
Balance = <span data-bind="style: { color: myBalance() < 0 ? 'red'
: 'black' }"><span data-bind="text:myBalance"></span></span>
<hr>
```

When we render again, Knockout renders the text as shown here:

```
My fourth KO uses Style binding:
Balance = -47.23
```

Managing visibility

To manage visibility of the elements in the ViewModel, use the following steps:

1. Add the following code to the ViewModel:

```
var viewModel = {
  myVariable: ko.observable()
  ,myHTML: ko.observable()
  ,myLeft: ko.observable()
  ,myRight: ko.observable()
  ,myBalance: ko.observable()
  ,isVisible: ko.observable()
}
```

2. Set the value of the `isVisible` variable after the binding of the ViewModel:

```
viewModel.myVariable("Awesome simple!");
viewModel.myHTML("<strong>Awesome</strong> simple!");
viewModel.myLeft("pullLeft");
viewModel.myRight("pushRight");
viewModel.myBalance(-47.23);
viewModel.isVisible(true);
```

3. Scripting can be a very powerful technique to use as your skills with Knockout advance. It can add a sense of automation and value to the user experience. Insert the following code after the `body` tag:

```
My fifth KO uses visible binding:
<div data-bind="visible: isVisible">Warning, the visible property
is set to true.</div>
<hr>
```

When we render again, Knockout renders the text as shown here. Try, of course, changing the value to `false` and run it again to see that it is working correctly for you.

> My fifth KO uses visible binding:
> Warning, the visible property is set to true.

Multibound control

The ViewModel does not need to be updated this time as the technique we are discussing is managed from the HTML DOM element side. We need to set the value of the `data-bind` variable for both color and text as follows:

```
viewModel.myVariable("Awesome simple!");
viewModel.myHTML("<strong>Awesome</strong> simple!");
```

Here, we explore our first `data-bind` where we are binding to more than one setting at the same time via the HTML markup. Using the bracketed form, we nest a slight amount of JavaScript right into the markup. Again, keep in mind that when you are using the JavaScript functionality you have to deal with the ViewModel attribute as a function and not as a variable. It is good to watch out for this as it is a common thing for new Knockout developers to overlook. Here is the code to add after the `body` tag:

```
My sixth KO uses multi-binding:
Balance = <span data-bind="style: { color: myBalance() < 0 ? 'red' :
'black' },text:myBalance"></span>
```

When we render again, Knockout renders the text shown here:

My sixth KO uses multi-binding: Balance = -47.23

Try changing the number and running it to get the number to show both black and red depending, of course, on having the right number setting in the code. You could even change the logic if you choose to.

Power development using browser developer tools

I suggest using the tools in Google Chrome for this book. The first tool that did a real good job was the Firefox tool called **Firebug**. Firebug is still a great tool, and the built-in developer tools in Firebug have made tremendous advances. You should also enjoy using the tools in Safari if you are a Mac user. If you are a die-hard fan of Internet Explorer, they have done a good job with the developer tools there as well. My point is, it is better to use developer tools everywhere, so don't make excuses to not use the developer tools in whatever browser you are using.

> If you happen to be working on or wanting to learn to build Chrome extensions and apps then here's how to enable developer mode. In the Chrome browser, click on the menu button next to the address bar. It is an icon with three lines stacked on top of each other. Under the selections on the side, click on **Extensions**, and you will see a checkbox at the top-right for **Developer mode**. Search on Google for more details as this is just a tip to whet your appetite.

When in Chrome, all you need to do to load the developer tools is press *F12* on a PC, and on a Mac use Command + *Alt* + *I*. You can also find them by looking under the Chrome menu. This button can be found on the right of the address bar as three stacked lines. Under **More tools** you will see the option for developer tools.

You can see it there for Windows, Mac, and even for the browser on the Chrome OS. When you click on it, the following window appears at the bottom of the browser:

We will not get into all the features of this tool because that would demand an entire book. We are just going to focus on a few key features, making it easier to debug your code while learning Knockout. You may want to undock the tools from the bottom of the browser. To do so, click on the pair of stacked boxes right next to the close (**x**) button at the upper right. This makes the tools appear in a separate window.

The console is the main thing we are interested in at the moment, so if you do not have it selected, click on it in the top bar of the developer tools. This gives you a prompt that looks very similar to a command-line prompt. When you start typing text, if there are variables or structures active in the browser DOM, it will bring it up with code hinting.

Select **viewModel** and then press the period. Notice that in the hinting there are all the model properties you created, listed with a few other variable settings. Select **viewModel.myHtml** and hit *Enter*. What you see is a function. To get the results you need to add parentheses to the end of the variable—for example, **viewModel.myHtml()**—and try again. You could retype it all, but you can also use the up and down arrows to cycle through recent command prompt entries if desired. This returns the value currently held in the ViewModel variable setting.

```
> viewModel.myHTML()
< "<strong>Awesome</strong> simple!"
>
```

Now we take it to the next level and use the same variable to change the value right from the command prompt. What we need to do is to watch the screen closely as we press the *Enter* key because we can see the power of having the data bound to the View through the ViewModel. Enter the following in the command prompt:

```
viewModel.myHTML("Knockout is <strong>Awesome</strong>!")
```

What you should see is the HTML of the second binding we entered updated automatically. That is a much easier way to work with the View than traditional JavaScript. For those who are wondering, it is also very compatible with jQuery. It can be used with all kinds of libraries though you should be careful to check them before considering them a match to make sure it is a good pair.

 You should also note that while we have been naming our ViewModel `viewModel`, it could be named any valid variable name. We are doing this just to help drive in the concept that this is our variable for the ViewModel.

Now let's use the balance in the calculation from the command console. Let's try entering the following:

```
viewModel.myBalance()*2
```

When we do, we should get -94.46 as the result, or another number if you entered in something different.

The Knockout debugger

This is what the Knockout context shows when you are in the **Elements** view:

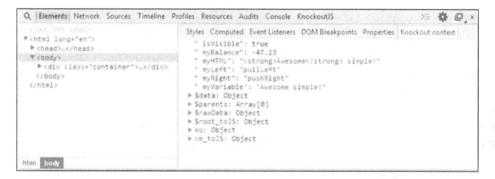

The add-in is available at the Chrome Web Store. It is a great store, and lots of the items worth getting are free. One of these items is the **KnockoutJS context debugger** which is released under an MIT license. The source code of this tool is on GitHub, which is very useful if you get large nested ViewModels. It has several features and provides great benefits when learning Knockout and building sites with it. To download this add-in use the following steps:

1. Go to `https://chrome.google.com/webstore/`.

2. Type `knockout` in the search box.

3. Under **Extensions** you should see **Knockoutjs context debugger** by timstuyckens.

Another thing that would help when working with Knockout or any data-binding library is the ability to trace what is going on. But this tool expands our reach beyond that ability. Select **KnockoutJS** from the top of the developer tools and you will see a button that says **Enable Tracing**. Click on it and go to the **Console** tab. Now enter the following code, and you will see all the changes to your DOM being dumped in the console window:

```
for(i=0;i<10;i++){viewModel.myBalance(1.1*i);}
```

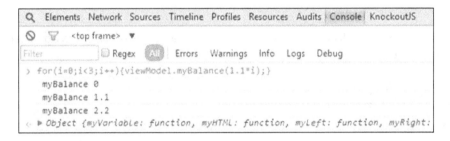

Shortcuts

While this may be a big gain for those who have never fired up the developer tools in a browser, let's look at a few things that could make working with the tools even better. One of those things is shortcuts. Right beside the button to open the tools in their own window or put them back in the footer section of the browser window, there is a **Settings** button. Click on it and you will see three side menu items. The last one is **Shortcuts**. Skim through this and it will help all shortcut lovers to do things even faster. You can also find a full list of the shortcuts at `https://developer.chrome.com/devtools/docs/shortcuts`, which you could print out or perhaps just bookmark the page.

The DOM inspection

In the browser window where we have the "LEFT" content wrapped in our `div` tag, right-click on it and select **Inspect Element**. (On a Mac, you can use double fingers to do the right-click.) This selects the element, and you will be able to see any `data-bind` attribute settings that might exist for that element as well as any other DOM features.

You can even play around with the DOM and double-click inside the elements panel to edit the DOM live. Live editing is one of my favorite features. What you need to understand is that the View binds to the ViewModel when you instantiate it via a script. You cannot change that by editing the DOM code in that panel. You can also edit the CSS and JavaScript on the page for testing and debugging in amazing ways and this, in my opinion, is a must-learn developer skill.

The AJAX inspection

It is an indispensable tool for me, when working with AJAX, to see what goes out and back using the **Network** Tab. You can see there is an XHR item in the listing, which allows you to view individual requests that arise while working on a page.

The resource inspection

We at SOSensible, my company, have built all kinds of web applications. One kind of web application allows the user to go offline with a web app. We needed to store the data in a browser-based database store and this tool let us inspect all those resources under the **Resources** tab.

The device emulation

In the bottom section of the developer tools, there is a section called drawer. If it is not showing, the menu buttons at the top-right have a button to hide or show the drawer. Once it is visible, you have a menu item for **Emulation**. This lets you refresh the screen to show a close emulation of what the view would be like on a particular device size and rotation.

There are a couple of items on the sidebar that also help with other features. There is a setting called **Device** to pick the device to emulate. There is a setting named **Screen** to manage the rotation and many other features you may want to customize. There is also **User Agent** to spoof the server into thinking it is a different device. Lastly, there is **Sensors** that allows you to set geolocation and accelerometer values.

Using internal functions with Knockout

The `applyBindings` method in the previously explained bindings section uses a common structure. We included that example in case you cross code written in that style. It will help you understand it if you see it someone else's code that is using that approach. Another style of coding is to declare the Model with a function declaration. The DOM markup or View code does not change for either scenario. Let's convert our binding example to a functional declaration. Copy the `binding.htm` file and create a new file called `functions.htm` in the same folder. Here is the original declaration:

```
var viewModel = {
  myVariable: ko.observable()
  ,myHTML: ko.observable()
  ,myLeft: ko.observable()
  ,myRight: ko.observable()
  ,myBalance: ko.observable()
  ,isVisible: ko.observable()
};
```

Note that we could have set the values of the observables immediately along with the declaration. If we had done that it would have looked like this:

```
var viewModel = {
  myVariable: ko.observable("Awesome simple!")
  ,myHTML: ko.observable("<strong>Awesome</strong> simple!")
  ,myLeft: ko.observable("pullLeft")
  ,myRight: ko.observable("pushRight")
  ,myBalance: ko.observable(-47.23)
  ,isVisible: ko.observable(true)
};
```

We are doing this to tighten our code for the sake of the book. You should use good logic when choosing which way to do this in your code. There are times where using this style of coding is important, but often it is just a matter of the coder's style. Beware of letting your style keep you from considering which one is best as you write the code.

Now we will look at moving the code over to a functional declaration. We start, of course, with a different kind of declaration because it is a function as appears here:

```
function viewModel() {
// add declarations here}
```

It would be equally valid to declare the ViewModel as follows. There is no significant difference:

```
viewModel = function() {
// add declarations here}
```

Now, we will look at adding our ViewModel items back in. In the structured approach we just described, the items were entered as collection items with the classic comma separator. In this model, each item is a parameter and is terminated by a semi-colon:

```
viewModel = function() {
this.myVariable = ko.observable("Awesome simple!");
this.myHTML = ko.observable("<strong>Awesome</strong>
  simple!");
this.myLeft = ko.observable("pullLeft");
this.myRight = ko.observable("pushRight");
this.myBalance = ko.observable(-47.23);
this.isVisible = ko.observable(true);}
```

Note that we declared each of these items with the `this` scope declaration, which refers to the ViewModel object. When programming in JavaScript, it is common practice to alias `this` to avoid scope confusion. We will rewrite the previous code one more time using `self` rather than `this` as the base scope:

```
viewModel = function() {
   var self = this;
self.myVariable = ko.observable("Awesome simple!");
self.myHTML = ko.observable("<strong>Awesome</strong>
  simple!");
self.myLeft = ko.observable("pullLeft");
self.myRight = ko.observable("pushRight");
self.myBalance = ko.observable(-47.23);
self.isVisible = ko.observable(true);}
```

 Note that we set the `self` variable using a var declaration. This prevents issues of external naming conflicts.

Now, if we run the page for `functions.htm` from our browser, it should run identical to our `binding.htm` file. Yet, there is a difference. This will help you understand why we introduced the developer tools where we did in the course. Open the tools and in the command prompt, enter `viewModel.isHTML()` to see what you get as a result:

```
> viewModel.myHTML()
⊗ ▶ TypeError: undefined is not a function
>
```

Preventing hidden features

In the previous screenshot we obtained the what you might think is an unexpected result as the View is obviously bound to the ViewModel. The issue here is an issue of the concept of **closure**. You are welcome to explore more about closure if you wish but just realize it means parts of an object or the item contents are there but hidden. When this type of declaration is made in this style, you cannot interact with it from JavaScript. The declaration should have been made with `new` to create an object from the function as follows:

```
ko.applyBindings(new viewModel());
```

If you run the browser and try to connect to the ViewModel now, you will see that it is still having the same issue with closure. We found this is the best way to work around it at my company:

```
vm = new viewModel();
ko.applyBindings(viewModel);
```

Now, we will reference the Model using `vm` rather than `viewModel` and this is the result we will get:

```
> vm.myHTML()
< "<strong>Awesome</strong> simple!"
>
```

We see that by declaring the object outside the argument passed to our Knockout `applyBindings` method, we avoided the closure issue. This is not an issue when using the structured style of ViewModel declaration. Hopefully, this saves you from hours of wondering what is wrong with your code or if Knockout is broken. We will not answer how much time I burned on this the first time it occurred, but it was long after I started using Knockout. It says that even experts can make rookie mistakes. I humbled myself and asked the community for help, and the answer came pretty fast.

Automating calculations with Knockout

In this section, we will take functions to a deeper level.

In the code bundle of chapter 1 do folder (`/ko_1/do/`), copy the `base.htm` file as `computed.htm` for this segment. After the leading `body` tag, put in the following View code:

```
<table>
    <tr>
        <th style="width:20%;">
            Item
```

```
        </th>
        <th style="width:40%;">
            Qty
        </th>
        <th>
            Price
        </th>
        <th>
            Tally
        </th>
    </tr>
    <tr>
        <td style="width:20%;">
            <em data-bind="text:item_1">Item</em>
        </td>
        <td style="width:40%;">
            <input type="text" data-bind="value:qty_1" />
        </td>
        <td>
            <span data-bind="text:price_1"></span>
        </td>
        <td>
            <span data-bind="text:tally_1"></span>
        </td>
    </tr>
</table>
```

Now we are ready to create the scripted side of the Knockout ViewModel code. Place this code inside the `script` tag after the KnockoutJS library is included:

```
calcModel = function(){
    var self = this;
    self.item_1 = ko.observable('Cell Phone');
    self.qty_1 =  ko.observable(0);
    self.price_1 = ko.observable(149.95);
    self.tally_1 = ko.computed(function(){
        var rslt = (+self.qty_1() * self.price_1()).toFixed(2);
        return rslt;
    },self);
}
vm = new calcModel();
ko.applyBindings(vm);
```

Notice that the computed function is now doing live calculations. We also added a fixed decimal position of two places. Enter a quantity to test:

Item	Qty	Price	Tally
Cell Phone	2	149.95	299.90

Create a second row of the table and the ViewModel that matches the features of the first row. I want you to create this on your own to make sure you are getting the skills as you go along here. You could, of course, peek at the example in the done folder, but you should try it on your own first.

Subtotal calculation

Now add this row to the bottom of the table to create a row for the subtotal. You can also see we created a cell in the table to tally the number of items in qty_1 and qty_2:

```
<tr>
    <td style="width:20%;">
         
    </td>
    <td style="width:40%;">
        <span data-bind="text:t_qty"></span>
    </td>
    <td>
        <em>subTotal</em>
    </td>
    <td>
        <span data-bind="text:subTotal"></span>
    </td>
</tr>
```

You also need to put the script code into the correct locations:

```
self.item_2 = ko.observable('Cell Case');
self.qty_2 = ko.observable(0);
self.price_2 = ko.observable(19.45);
self.tally_2 = ko.computed(function(){
    var rslt = (+self.qty_2() * self.price_2()).toFixed(2);
    return rslt;
},self);
self.t_qty = ko.computed(function(){
    return +(self.qty_1()) + +(self.qty_2());
},self);
```

```
self.subTotal = ko.computed(function(){
    var rslt = (+(self.tally_1()) + +(self.tally_2())).toFixed(2);
    return rslt;
});
```

You may have noticed that we placed an extra + before some of the variables. This is a standard JavaScript approach to making sure the number entered into the input box comes out as a number. In some browsers and some conditions the number is the string representation of the number. The addition of + solves this issue.

Now run the page and enter the quantity to ensure that all of your calculations are working:

Item	Qty		Price	Tally
Cell Phone	2		149.95	299.90
Cell Case	2		19.45	38.90
	4		*subTotal*	338.80

Tax time

What fun would buying things be without paying taxes? Well, either way it is a function we all need to get right. Add the following code to the table to have a row for taxes:

```
<tr>
    <td style="width:20%;">
         
    </td>
    <td style="width:40%;">
        ( rate  in decimal <input data-bind="value: taxRate;"
/> )
    </td>
    <td>
        <em>Tax</em>
    </td>
    <td>
        <span data-bind="text:taxed"></span>
    </td>
</tr>
```

Now add the code here to the `script` section of the page to make our ViewModel run smartly. Our goal is not to write the most efficient code in all of the world but rather to expose you to learning to think the Knockout way:

```
self.tax = ko.observable(.05);
self.taxed = ko.computed(function(){
    return +(self.subTotal()*self.tax()).toFixed(2);
});
self.taxRate = ko.computed({
    read: function(){
        return self.tax()*100 + '%';
    },
    write: function(value){
        value = parseFloat(value.replace(/[^\.\d]/g, ""));
        self.tax(+value/100);
    }
});
```

If we were coding the page with standard JavaScript or even with jQuery to get the amount of functionality we have achieved, it would take many multiples of the code we have on the page here. This approach is far more elegant and much smaller.

Notice how our `taxRate` is done just a little differently. Calculation functions in Knockout can read and write. You can also call other external resources because it is standard script code. Note that in our scripted code we have to place the values in parentheses to do the assignments as we did to the tax value.

You should also notice that we are converting the value in and out of decimal format and adding a percentage to the displayed value of the taxes in the input box. It also smartly strips the percent mark off if you enter it when updating the tax rate.

 Regular expressions like the one used in our `write` method are a way to supercharge your apps. Make it a point to learn at least basic regular expressions. If you do not know how to do the advanced stuff, you can often find what you need either in a Google search, or some "happy guru" will volunteer to assist you with a winning answer in some online forum.

Refresh the page with the updates, and you will see that even the actual tax amount has been calculated in the **Tally** column:

Item	Qty	Price	Tally
Cell Phone	3	149.95	449.85
Cell Case	2	19.45	38.90
	5	*subTotal*	488.75
	(rate in decimal 5.5%) *Tax*		26.88

Final total

Here we have the final segment of the View code for our calculation example:

```
<tr>
    <td style="width:20%;">
         
    </td>
    <td style="width:40%;">
         
    </td>
    <td>
        <em>Total</em>
    </td>
    <td>
        <span data-bind="text:total"></span>
    </td>
</tr>
```

The last piece of script code should be added to the ViewModel. There is nothing fancy about this section of code other than its ability to complete our functionality. We add in the value of the taxed item here, and again, we wrap the numbers with a parentheses and use the `toFixed` function to set the answer to two decimal places.

```
self.total = ko.computed(function(){
    var rslt = (+self.subTotal() + self.taxed()).toFixed(2);
    return rslt;
});
```

Now we can run the code and play with the entry boxes to see that everything is working as expected. For new developers, it may not surprise you to see how little code it takes to make a page like this work. It used to take so much code that hardly anyone anywhere would take the time to attempt building tools like this. It was compounded because things worked differently from one browser to the next. While this is still true, libraries like Knockout remove many of those pains and let us concentrate on the results instead of the platforms.

Running the code now should give us results similar to this screen capture:

Item	Qty	Price	Tally
Cell Phone	5	149.95	749.75
Cell Case	4	19.45	77.80
	9	subTotal	827.55
	(rate in decimal 4.5%) Tax		37.24
		Total	864.79

Working with non-Knockout functions

Now, we will add an external function to show an alternate way to format values in the View. You are going to make one more pass at modifying the `computed.htm` example we just worked on. First at the top of the script, add a function with the following code:

```
dollarFormat = function(value){
    return "$ "+value;
}
```

Now go into the View and change the final total as follows. Test it to make sure you got it right and then change all of them if you desire:

```
<span data-bind="text:dollarFormat(total())"></span>
```

This is what the page looks like with the last item formatted as a dollar amount:

Item	Qty	Price	Tally
Cell Phone	5	149.95	749.75
Cell Case	5	19.45	97.25
	10	subTotal	847.00
	(rate in decimal 5%) Tax		42.35
		Total	$ 889.35

We could have added an external function that is used inside a calculation to show its use inside the ViewModel. You are still left with some work to do as you will have to choose the best place to put things like that. Perhaps, in a couple of versions, these tools will just magically do it all for us. Well, even if they did, there will be new needs and we will still have a good opportunity to solve issues through code for those we serve.

Summary

You now have a taste of the benefits of KnockoutJS. This is just the beginning of the power of KnockoutJS. The benefit of Knockout is that it solves problems that libraries like jQuery do not solve, and yet has the ability to work side by side if needed. Knockout provides both binding and functional intelligence that automate and simplify HTML and coding the same way jQuery simplifies JavaScript coding.

In the next chapter we will build on this knowledge by learning how to use conditional binding, observable arrays, simplifying nested items, and some keys on how to work with collections.

2
Using Arrays, Nesting, and Grids

Now we've had a taste of KnockoutJS, we are now ready to learn new coding skills. In this chapter, we will see how to extend our MVVM skills to make a lot more sweet data interaction experiences. This chapter will focus on:

- Conditional binding
- Simpler nested binding
- Observable arrays
- Paged grids
- Sorting data collections

Conditional binding

Data binding is the essence of many new libraries that interact with the HTML markup as it gets converted to the DOM. We saw binding in *Chapter 1, Getting Started with KnockoutJS*, using the `data-bind ="..."` bindings. Here we will be looking at conditional binding.

The first thing we will do is understand the concept of conditional binding. Our example is meant to be conceptual. We will show a more practical example shortly in this chapter.

The `if` binding plays a very similar role to the visible property in the DOM. The difference is that the `if` binding actually adds and removes the content from the DOM whereas visible swaps the CSS display style between visible and none.

Create a new file by copying the _base.htm file, located in the ko_2/do folder, and naming it condition.htm within the do folder. If you get stuck, there is a completed copy inside the done folder. To make things look better, we will now be using the larger Bootstrap template base as it will give us better presentation. You will see the following area in the markup code, which is where you will place the code for the rest of the book:

```
<!--
markup code here
-->
```

You will place the rest of the code in the same place as explained in *Chapter 1, Getting Started with KnockoutJS*. Again, this is just to make our work look better as we go through the rest of the book. Now, enter the following code in the markup section of the htm file:

```
<label><input type="checkbox" data-bind="checked:
showDetails" /> Include Condition</label>
 
<span data-bind="if:showDetails">
    ( This section shows when the condition is
selected. )
</span>
```

This will give us a checkbox to toggle our content. We will create a variable called showDetails to bind our content toggle in the script section of the page. When the checkbox is checked, the content will be added, and when the checkbox is unchecked, the content will be removed. Here is the content for the script section of the .htm file:

```
myVM = {
    showDetails: ko.observable(false)
}
ko.applyBindings(myVM);
```

There is nothing complex here. We just have a variable that will hold our true or false state. When the variable is true, the content will be added, and when the variable is false, it will be removed from the page. Here is what it will look like when the value is true:

☑ **Include Condition** (This section shows when the condition is selected.)

Go ahead and run the code in the browser and toggle the content by setting the checkbox as checked and not checked a few times to make sure your code is working.

Introduction to arrays in Knockout

We will start by working with an unbound array. You will see that Knockout is smart enough to still work with the array and display the contents correctly. In fact, the array we will start out with will be an array with nested data. Add the highlighted data to the script section of our page:

```
myVM = {
showDetails: ko.observable(false),
employee: [
{name:"John Jones", spouse: { name: "Mary Jones"}},
{name:"Bill Williams", spouse: null},
{name:"Sandy Rivers", spouse: { name: "Mark Rivers"}},
]
}
```

The employee array data will automatically bind to the MVVM system when we run our applyBindings function on the page. We will need some markup to tell us that it has actually worked. I suggest separating the section of content on the page using the <hr/> tag just for clarity. Now add the following code to the markup section:

```
<ul data-bind="foreach: employee">
    <li>Employee: <strong data-bind="text:name"></strong>
        <div data-bind="if: spouse">( Spouse: <strong data-
bind="text: spouse.name"></strong> )</div>
        <div data-bind="ifnot: spouse">( AVAILABLE )</div>
    </li>
</ul>
```

We learn a few new commands now with Knockout. The first is the foreach command. If we have an array, which I refer to as a collection, this will look through each item. We tell the foreach loop to loop through the employee array collection.

The next thing you will notice is that the elements of the collection are addressed at the item level. In other words, we do not need to use myVM.employee.name; instead, we simply use name. This makes for much cleaner code.

You will also see we are using the `if` command again. We have also thrown in the opposite logic command, `ifnot`. If a null result is returned, then it is understood to be the same thing functionally as a false value. This means if a person does not have a spouse, they will be marked as available. Hint: this would likely cause social waves if you ran a page in your company declaring who was available, so this is definitely not suggested as the best practice for a company web page.

- Employee: **John Jones**
  (Spouse: **Mary Jones**)
- Employee: **Bill Williams**
  (AVAILABLE)
- Employee: **Sandy Rivers**
  (Spouse: **Mark Rivers**)

When we run the code, we get the result as shown in the preceding screenshot. We see that Bill is not married as expected. Since we know it would not be a good idea to post that someone is available there is a simpler way to display this same information while skipping the risky classification. We will copy the code section and repeat it using the `with` command in place of the `if` command as follows:

```
<ul data-bind="foreach: employee">
    <li>Employee: <strong data-bind="text:name"></strong>
        <div data-bind="with: spouse">( Spouse: <strong data-
bind="text:name"></strong> )</div>
    </li>
</ul>
```

Here is what the page looks like when we run the `with` command:

- Employee: **John Jones**
  (Spouse: **Mary Jones**)
- Employee: **Bill Williams**
- Employee: **Sandy Rivers**
  (Spouse: **Mark Rivers**)

Now I am not saying that `with` is safer than `if` from a technical perspective. You will need to think through your business logic smartly just like you would think about the social issues in this example. Take a few moments and think about the business requirements as the issues that are there are not always technical issues. We need to make sure the technical code is taking care of any business issues that we should know about as we do our work.

Working with array collections

Let's copy our `_base.htm` file to `arrays.htm` in the do folder to continue our study of array collections in Knockout. First, add our core markup to the new page as follows:

```
<ul data-bind="foreach: employee">
    <li>Employee: <strong data-bind="text:name"></strong>
        <div data-bind="if: spouse">( Spouse: <strong data-
  bind="text: spouse.name"></strong> )</div>
    </li>
</ul>
```

We will again need to create a data model in the `script` section for this to work. The following is the code for the data section. Here is where we will start using an observable array. Knockout uses additional logic to handle arrays than it does for simple variable types. These arrays can be a collection of simple variables or nested rows of complex structure:

```
myVM = {
    showDetails: ko.observable(false),
    employee: ko.observableArray([
            {name:'John Jones', spouse: { name: "Mary Jones"}},
            {name:'Bill Williams', spouse: null},
            {name:'Sandy Rivers', spouse: { name: "Mark Rivers"}}
    ]),
    alt: ko.observableArray()
}
ko.applyBindings(myVM);
```

Run the page and make sure you get the following result. Of course, if you modified the data, you get bonus points for exploring and enjoying the work. In that case, your results will look slightly different.

- Employee: **John Jones**
  (Spouse: **Mary Jones**)
- Employee: **Bill Williams**
- Employee: **Sandy Rivers**
  (Spouse: **Mark Rivers**)

We will be adding four different buttons to experience working with array collections using observable arrays in Knockout. Before we do that, here are the functions we can perform on array methods:

Function	Description
push()	Adds item to the end of the collection
pop()	Removes the last item from the collection
unshift()	Inserts a new item at the start of the collection
shift()	Removes the first item from the collection and returns it
reverse()	Swaps the order of items in the collection
sort()	Sorts the order of the collection (requires a sorting function)
splice()	Removes a given number of elements from the collection beginning at a declared starting point
remove()	Removes all values that equal something and returns them as an array; this can also be run as a function for identifying items
removeAll()	Removes all items from an array list or removes everything and returns removed items as an array
destroy()	This the **Ruby on Rails** (**RoR**) version of remove() to make things more familiar to RoR developers
destroyAll()	This is the RoR version of removeAll() to make things more familiar to RoR developers

We will start by adding a button to the page to work with reversing the array collection order. On this page, we will be practicing interacting with the data model by using functions outside the MVVM binding of Knockout. We will still be interacting with the binding results. This will help build inside and outside coding skills to use Knockout in different scenarios. Use the following code to make a button:

```
<button onclick="myVM.employee.reverse()">Reverse Sort
    Staff</button>
```

You see here that we are running the JavaScript directly from the button using the reverse method of the array collection. Add this button and run the page again. After clicking on the button, you will see that all of the items in the array collection are now in reverse order. Click on it again and again and you will see it will reverse the items each time you click. If you compare the previous screenshot with the following screenshot, you can see the items in the array collection are reversed:

- Employee: **Sandy Rivers**
  (Spouse: **Mark Rivers**)
- Employee: **Bill Williams**
- Employee: **John Jones**
  (Spouse: **Mary Jones**)

Reverse Sort Staff

While this is all nice, dynamic websites are sites that need to have data added and removed. We will get started learning about this right now in this chapter. The first thing we will do is create a button to add staff. Add the highlighted code here to the markup section of the page:

```
<button onclick="myVM.employee.reverse()">Reverse Sort Staff</button>
 
<button onclick="addStaff()">Add Staff</button>
```

- Employee: **John Jones**
  (Spouse: **Mary Jones**)
- Employee: **Bill Williams**
- Employee: **Sandy Rivers**
  (Spouse: **Mark Rivers**)

Reverse Sort Staff   Add Staff

You see the `addStaff` function that we need to add staff to our page attached to the `onClick` event handler of the button. We will need to use the `push` method of our bound array collection to add this in. Add the following function to the `script` section of the code:

```
function addStaff(){
    myVM.employee.push({name:"Charlie Targus", spouse:
  {name:"Patti Targus"}});
}
```

Now, when we run the code, it should add the new employee as expected. The `push` method will always add the item to the end of the collection, as seen in the following screenshot:

Let's refresh the page and follow these steps in order to verify that assumption:

1. Refresh the page.
2. Click on the **Reverse Sort Staff** button.
3. Click on the **Add Staff** button.
4. Click on the **Reverse Sort Staff** button one more time.

And here is the output image you get:

If all we wanted to do was put the item at the top of the list, it would have been too much work. This will become especially true as we begin to work with larger and larger sets of data. To insert an item at the start of the array collection, we will use the `unshift` method in place of the `push` method.

Now is there anyone besides me who thinks the term `unshift()` is just strange? Perhaps that will help us remember it easier!

Removing the last item

We saw how `push` added the item to the end of the data; now we can take a look at pulling the last item off the array collection. If you use the `pop` method, it will not be the last item added to the end of the data, but the last item on the collection. This will be the last item showing on the page at the bottom of the list of employees; in our case, we will use the following lines code:

```
<br/>
<button onclick="myVM.employee.pop()">Remove Staff</button>
```

Now add a staff member using the **Add Staff** button and you will get the following result:

We see things working just like before. Now there are four staff members. We are now going to remove the last item using the inline JavaScript code within our button's `onClick` method. This has the opposite effect of the `push` function that adds an item to the end of the array collection. It removes the very last item of the array collection.

Here is the view you should have after clicking on the **Remove Staff** button:

Try clicking on the **Reverse Sort Staff** button followed by the **Remove Staff** button. This time, you should see **John Jones** gone from the bottom of the list, and the list should look like this:

Sorting time

Displaying data is a very common use case for web pages. Perhaps the most common function people perform on data besides searching is sorting. We are going to look at how to sort data based on particular data fields. This time, we will create the logic first. Enter the following code into the `script` tag:

```
function doSort() {
    myVM.employee.sort(function (left, right) {
        return left.name == right.name ? 0 : (left.name <
    right.name ? -1 : 1);
    });
}
```

We will break down the logic for those unfamiliar with this level of JavaScript:

1. The `sort` function passes in two structures. Each structure matches the items being sorted. The variable name could be anything; we choose `left` and `right` because it helps the programmer remember which variable is which. You can use, of course, any variable naming you choose. Each variable contains the whole structure of the item being passed in.

2. The basic return value for `sort` needs to be true or false. This tells the program whether the two items should be swapped. This is why they return a value using the ternary symbols. It is likely that these are not symbols you used in high school math, so they will be foreign to most of us. Here is an explanation:

   ○ First, there is a logical comparison followed by the ? symbol; symbolizing the value before ? tells us whether the results should be based on true or on false.

- ○ The first value is what should be returned if the results are true.
- ○ Then there is a colon to represent the results that should be returned if the logic evaluation is false.

 You should see here that the logic can be stacked to perform a second logical evaluation if desired. This could be in either the true or false position.

3. The second value will be what is returned if the value is false. Again, in this example, we observe a nested logic that is run when the results are false.

   Here is the same logic in an `if` statement for the sake of comparison:

```
function doSort() {
    myVM.employee.sort(function (left, right) {
        if (left.name == right.name) {
            return 0;
        } else {
            if (left.name < right.name) {
                return -1;
            } else {
                return 1;
            }
        }
    });
}
```

4. One of the things you should notice is that there is definitely less code using the ternary operator approach. This doesn't mean using the `if` approach is wrong; it's just more code to get right, and the more code we type, of course, the more time we are likely to spend debugging. If you don't have a standard where you work and prefer to use the `if` logic, feel free to go that way. My main goal was to show you what many experienced developers do so you could understand the code.

5. Now, let's add the button to call the code in the markup:

```
<br/>
<button onclick="myVM.employee.pop()">Remove Staff</button>
 
<button onclick="doSort()">Sort Staff</button>
```

This is what you should see before the sort button is clicked on:

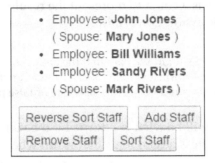

Notice that it sorts alphabetically based on the first name because the whole name is stored as a single field. This is what we expected, and it is working correctly if it looks the same as in the following image:

6. Now, let's add a staff member to see whether it will sort properly with the added item:

7. Press the **Sort Staff** button to see whether our added item appears properly in the employee list:

The simpleGrid plugin

Just like jQuery allows for custom plugins, it is possible to use plugins with Knockout as well. Here, we are going to use a simple plugin to add grid functionality to our page. This plugin also smartly adds paging to the page. We will also do some simple CSS to set our grid so it loosens up the space between the cells in the table.

The reason we code with jQuery, KnockoutJS, Bootstrap, and other **Don't Repeat Yourself (DRY)** libraries is that they package our work. We don't have to rethink, recode, or repeat our work when this is done. Using solutions such as jQuery and KnockoutJS, we can DRY out our code by adding our own library extensions. The simple grid plugin is an example of this.

Note that we will cover enough detail in this book that by the end you should be able to modify this plugin or build your own. However, you will have to understand JavaScript, CSS, HTML, and other topics enough to get the job you are seeking to DRY out. Regarding KnockoutJS, you will get the knowledge you need from this book. (The simpleGrid code was acquired from the KnockoutJS main site. It is not part of the core but great learning code just the same.)

Use the `_base.htm` copy and create a new page in the do folder of ko_2, named paged.htm for this exercise. The first modification we will make is adding the highlighted line after the include tag for Knockout.js near the bottom of the code:

```
<script src="/share/js/knockout.js"></script>
<script src="/share/js/simplegrid.js"></script>
<script>
</script>
```

This adds in the logic we need for the simple grid plugin for Knockout. Now we can create the markup for our exercise. In the markup section, add the following markup:

```
<div data-bind="simpleGrid: orderVM"></div>
<button data-bind="click: addOrder">Add Order</button>
<button data-bind="click: orderPageOne, enable:
  orderVM.currentPageIndex">First Page</button>
```

Look closely at the `data-bind` attribute of the `div` tag. You should notice a new command attribute called `simpleGrid`. This is not part of Knockout by default. It has been added by our plugin. The `orderVM` attribute that follows is a root structure in our ViewModel. This elegant code teaches you how to package your code. It is so much simpler and easier to reuse your work or even take advantage of the work of others.

Let's go through this code. First, we will add in some data for the grid within the `script` tag section. This code will be a standard array collection. Take a look at the following code:

```
var initOrders = [
    { name: "John Jones", item: "Apples", qty: 12 },
    { name: "Bill Williams", item: "Pears", qty: 24 },
    { name: "Sandy Rivers", item: "Bananas", qty: 44 },
    { name: "Patti Targus", item: "Peaches", qty: 12 }
];
```

Next, we will add our ViewModel to bind using Knockout. Add the following code to the page in the `script` section:

```
var PagedOrderModel = function (orders) {
    this.orders = ko.observableArray(orders);
    this.orderVM = new ko.simpleGrid.viewModel({
        data: this.orders
    });
};
ko.applyBindings(new PagedOrderModel(initOrders));
```

Running the code

This is a common manner in which you will see code for Knockout. Let's run the code and make some observations:

name	item	qty
John Jones	Apples	12
Bill Williams	Pears	24
Sandy Rivers	Bananas	44
Patti Targus	Peaches	12
Page: 1		

We see that our data displays as expected with the names of the collection item fields listed as the column names. It also added a paging item to the bottom automatically. This is the default configuration when running the code for the `simpleGrid` plugin. The default page size is 5 records per page. Notice that the columns are all squished together. Let's begin by adding the following line of code to the CSS styles on our page:

```
table { width: 400px;}
```

name	item	qty
John Jones	Apples	12
Bill Williams	Pears	24
Sandy Rivers	Bananas	44
Patti Targus	Peaches	12
Page: 1		

This looks much better with this simple modification. If you are using this grid and actually need more control over the style, you can use the cascading logic in CSS and nest the table inside a second `div` tag to create an ID or class to manage tables contained within that class.

Next, we want to modify the columns and the default number of columns that show by setting the configuration. Add this highlighted code to our `script` section on the page:

```
this.orderVM = new ko.simpleGrid.viewModel({
    data: this.orders,
    columns: [
            { headerText: "Customer", rowText: "name"},
            { headerText: "Item", rowText: "item"},
            { headerText: "Count", rowText: "qty"}
    ],
    pageSize: 3
});
```

With the columns detail declared and the page size set, we see the greater value of using DRY code. This has enabled us to manage the ViewModel from our scripted code. This is our result with our code at this point:

Customer	Item	Count
John Jones	Apples	12
Bill Williams	Pears	24
Sandy Rivers	Bananas	44
Page: 1 2		

Now you can click through to page 2 to see how this grid is working. We also see that our columns look much better with custom column names.

It is time to consider the best practice approach to coding with Knockout. Open your browser developer tools and go to **Console**. From the console, we want to interact with the ViewModel. Try typing the following in the command prompt:

```
> PagedOrderModel.orders()
```

You will get a response similar to the undefined response given by Chrome. The model is there and working but suddenly you cannot access the model. This one stumped me the first time my code had this issue. The biggest stump was that my code came from an online example, but there was a key point I was missing. The online example was not interacting with the code from the command prompt and it was not interacting with the code from JavaScript outside the ViewModel.

The problem is when we declare a new object within a JavaScript function, the object will not be available outside the call to the code. We can solve this by creating a variable to hold the object outside the method call and then passing in the object that was created outside the method argument. Let's change the applyBindings method by making the following changes. First add the line declaring the variable and then update the applyBindings method, as follows:

```
pagedOrderModel = new PagedOrderModel(initOrders);
ko.applyBindings(pagedOrderModel);
```

Now we can return to the browser developer tools and run the page again. Then type the new command in and notice that the first P is now in lowercase. JavaScript is case sensitive, so make sure you get your upper and lowercase right:

```
> pagedOrderModel.orders()
```

Now you should see an array of collection items. I expanded the first one so we could see the results from Chrome here:

```
>  pagedOrderModel.orders()
   [▼ Object                    ,  ▶ Object , ▶ Object , ▶ Object ]
         item: "Apples"
         name: "John Jones"
         qty: 12
        ▶ __proto__: Object
```

If you are using JavaScript and it is not connecting to your ViewModel, then you might want to make sure you have not made the previously explained error in coding. This is only an issue if you need to connect to the ViewModel from outside the ViewModel.

Now it is time to add some buttons below our grid for even more custom control. We will be adding two buttons: **Add Order** and **First Page**. Let's add the **Add Order** button first. It is code we should be familiar with as we have used it earlier in this chapter. We are going to use it again to show that even while working with a completely different **user interface (UI)** presentation, when we update the data in the ViewModel, the View is automatically updated. Add the following code to our `script` section on the page:

```
this.addOrder = function(){
        this.orders.push({name:"Gerry Markus", item: "Plums",
   qty:20});
};
```

We also, of course, need the markup for the button:

```
<button data-bind="click: addOrder">Add Order</button>
```

After adding the button, refresh the browser. Add the order and click through to the second page of data, and this is what it should look like:

Customer	Item	Count
Patti Targus	Peaches	12
Gerry Markus	Plums	20
Page: 1 2		
Add Order		

We see that the record for **Gerry Markus** has been added. We could use any of the code we used in earlier examples to do things like reversing or removing records using the array methods listed in this chapter.

Now, we have one more button to add that will allow us to control the grid page from our ViewModel. First, add the following markup:

```
<button data-bind="click: orderPageOne">First Page</button>
```

We see the click event is wired to the ViewModel method to move to page one. We also see a command to enable the page index. This will make sure our index is updated.

There are some other methods that can be called on `simpleGrid` that have been listed here. You will notice that some of the items are variables while others are method calls:

- `pagedOrderModel.orderVM.columns`
- `pagedOrderModel.orderVM.data()`
- `pagedOrderModel.orderVM.currentPageIndex()`
- `pagedOrderModel.orderVM.itemsOnCurrentPage()`
- `pagedOrderModel.orderVM.maxPageIndex()`
- `pagedOrderModel.orderVM.pageSize`

Remember, if you use these items bound to the Knockout `data-bind` attributes, you don't always need the parenthesis. This topic was covered in *Chapter 1, Getting Started with KnockoutJS*.

The final `script` section should look like this:

```
var PagedOrderModel = function(orders) {
    this.orders = ko.observableArray(orders);
    this.addOrder = function(){
            this.orders.push({name:"Gerry Markus", item: "Plums",
  qty:20});
};
    this.orderPageOne = function(){
            this.orderVM.currentPageIndex(0);
};
    this.orderVM = new ko.simpleGrid.viewModel({
            data: this.orders,
            columns: [
                    { headerText: "Customer", rowText: "name"},
                    { headerText: "Item", rowText: "item"},
                    { headerText: "Count", rowText: "qty"}
            ],
            pageSize: 3
    });
};
```

Final sort

Congratulations on creating a fairly functional piece of code using Knockout! Yet, what would data interaction be without the ability to sort? We are going to see how to take the sorting we did earlier and modify it to make it more dynamic than our previous example with a few simple modifications. You can just continue to modify the current page or you could copy the page as `sorting.htm` as that is how we approached it. Note that this is completely a matter of choice as it will only serve to make your `do` folder match our `done` folder.

Add the following two buttons to your page:

```
<button data-bind="click: sort('name')">Sort By Name</button>
<button data-bind="click: sort('item')">Sort By Item</button>
```

In our previous example for sorting, we did not pass in any values during the method call. Here, we are passing the name of a field in our data that tells us what we will be sorting with. This follows our theme of DRY coding as we are able to use the same command for either of these buttons or in any future code that matches. Here is the `script` code we need to add to actually do the sorting:

```
this.sort = function(by){
    this.orders.sort(function(left,right){
        return left[by] < right[by] ? -1 : 1;
    });
};
```

As simple as it seems, this is all the code it takes to create a reusable piece of code allowing us to sort when desired. Here is a screenshot showing name-based sorting:

Customer	Item	Count
Bill Williams	Pears	24
John Jones	Apples	12
Patti Targus	Peaches	12

Page: 1 2

Add Order	First Page
Sort By Name	Sort By Item

Here is another screenshot based on item sorting:

Customer	Item	Count
John Jones	Apples	12
Sandy Rivers	Bananas	44
Patti Targus	Peaches	12

Page: 1 2

Add Order	First Page
Sort By Name	Sort By Item

Why don't you create one more button to sort based on quantity as an exercise to see whether you have it figured out. The following screenshot is what the table should look like if you get it right. We will do one more thing though. We need to make sure our sort is out of order, so click on the **Sort By Name** button first. Then, clicking on the **Sort By Quantity** button should give us this result:

Customer	Item	Count
Patti Targus	Peaches	12
John Jones	Apples	12
Bill Williams	Pears	24

Page: 1 2

Add Order	First Page	
Sort By Name	Sort By Item	Sort By Quantity

Now, we should modify the table so that we can do reverse sorting. Basically, all that is needed is for us to flip our greater than sign in our code where we compare the left and right items passed from the sorting logic. We will, of course, also need another argument in our method because we want to reuse our code. Since the sort direction is not always passed in, we will also include a line to set ascending sort as the default choice if one is not declared. The `script` code should look like this with the changes highlighted:

```
this.sort = function (by, direction) {
    direction = typeof direction === 'undefined' ?
        'asc' : direction
    if (direction === 'asc') {
        this.orders.sort(function (left, right) {
            return left[by] < right[by] ? -1 : 1;
        });
```

```
    } else {
        this.orders.sort(function (left, right) {
            return left[by] > right[by] ? -1 : 1;
        });
    }
};
```

We will, of course, need a new set of buttons for the reverse sort as well:

```
<button data-bind="click: sort('name','desc')">Reverse By
    Name</button>
<button data-bind="click: sort('item','desc')">Reverse By
    Item</button>
<button data-bind="click: sort('qty','desc')">Reverse By
    Quantity</button>
```

Here is the view with the reverse sort on the quantity column labeled **Count**:

Customer	Item	Count
Sandy Rivers	Bananas	44
Bill Williams	Pears	24
Patti Targus	Peaches	12

Page: 1 2

Add Order | First Page

Sort By Name | Sort By Item | Sort By Quantity

Reverse By Name | Reverse By Item | Reverse By Quantity

Summary

If you have ever built any JavaScript pages with this much interaction with your data using JavaScript or even with jQuery, then you will know why the library deserves the title of Knockout. The amount of power we have gained using this library in just two chapters is compelling. Through this chapter you should have gained the ability to do conditional binding, nested binding, observable array collections, adding and deleting records in array style management, and sorting observable arrays. You even got a quick look at a Knockout plugin.

In the next chapter, we will learn to drive web forms with the power of Knockout. They think differently; and for a few, that is the first reaction. It is an interesting double take as the second reaction that nearly instantly follows is that it is better. Event binding is also a topic we will dig into in the next chapter with special focus on the over-the-top punch Knockout gives us when dealing with grid forms.

3
Giving Forms the Knockout Touch

Two of the oldest uses of the web are sharing and gathering information. This exchange includes the use of form and non-form elements. In this chapter, we will learn how to streamline coding and user interaction using the following focus areas:

- Event binding
- Text binding
- The textInput binding
- Web 3.0
- Radio and checkbox binding
- Select binding
- Grid forms

Event binding

Let me start off by saying that I have not tested every type of event that can be bound to Knockout, but there are tons of events in HTML, or rather DOM, that can be tested. It seems with HTML5-friendly browsers the number of the browsers available to us has increased. I would suggest that you make sure that you test to validate if any newer events are actually available on the platform you are targeting.

When we bind an event it requires a handler. These handlers are either functions or methods on objects. The functions can be part of the ViewModel or external to the scope of the ViewModel. As a reminder, when functions are part of the ViewModel we can assign the function method without ( ). If we are passing arguments then we would, of course, use them, even if they were part of the ViewModel.

Common events we would look for in the View would include click, keypress, mouseover, and mouseout. There are many other events, but that is enough of a list to give you an idea of what events are, if this is a new concept to you.

The binding markup

We will start by creating the HTML for our page. Create a file named enable.html for this example:

```
<div>
  <div data-bind="event: { mouseover: oneLeft }">
    Move One Left
  </div>
  <div data-bind="event: { mouseover: oneRight }">
    Move One Right
  </div>
  <div style="border:solid 1px black;">
    <div data-bind="css: oneClass">
      ( One )
    </div>
    <div data-bind="css: twoClass">
      ( Two )
    </div>
    <div style="clear:both;"></div>
  </div>
  <button data-bind="event: {mousedown: twoLeft }">Move Two
  Left</button>
  <button data-bind="event: {mouseup: twoRight }">Move Two
  Right</button>
</div>
```

We see the data-bind attribute has an event declaration in this code. We are going to bind the two first elements to the mouseover event. oneLeft is a function that the binding calls when the mouse is over the element. We see again that ( ) is not needed because we will be creating the function as part of the ViewModel.

The middle two div tags here have the element's class, the CSS attribute, set by the Knockout data-bind attribute. This would be a good time for us to create our extra classes before we do the code side of the work. Here is the CSS code:

```
<style type="text/css">
.putLeft { float:left; }
.putRight { float:right; }
</style>
```

These are two very simple float classes. The first two declarations in our ViewModel will be observables holding the value of our classes assigned to these elements. Note that we are declaring these as classes, so do not start the class name with a period. The CSS assumes this is the case.

```
<script>
    var vm = {
        oneClass: ko.observable('putLeft'),
        twoClass: ko.observable('putLeft'),
        /* mode code coming */
    };
</script>
```

If we look back at our HTML markup code, we see the events are not mouseover but rather mousedown and mouseup. These ViewModel event handlers, also known as functions, will call the methods to manage the **(Two)** item in the box on the browser page. Let's add the code for both sets of handlers:

```
oneLeft: function() {
    this.oneClass('putLeft');
},
oneRight: function() {
    this.oneClass('putRight');
},
twoLeft: function() {
    this.twoClass('putLeft');
},
twoRight: function() {
    this.twoClass('putRight');
}
```

All we are doing is changing the text of the ViewModel elements as this will change the bound CSS to match. This will, of course, shift the assigned element to float left or right on the page. Here is the complete code for this example:

```
< script >
var vm = {
    oneClass: ko.observable('putLeft'),
    twoClass: ko.observable('putLeft'),
    oneLeft: function () {
        this.oneClass('putLeft');
    },
    oneRight: function () {
        this.oneClass('putRight');
    },
```

```
        twoLeft: function () {
            this.twoClass('putLeft');
        },
        twoRight: function () {
            this.twoClass('putRight');
        }
    };
    ko.applyBindings(vm); < /script>
```

Now run the code in the browser and you should see the **(One)** element shifting left and right when hovering over the items above the box. You will have to actually click the items below the box to get them to take action.

```
Move One Left
Move One Right
( One )( Two )
Move Two Left    Move Two Right
```

It would be great if we could get the book to show you the results. Perhaps in e-books in the future that will be possible, but for now we will stay old school and actually enter the code and test it.

The binding checkbox with visibility

In this example we will create a file named event.html and copy the _base.html to save time. We will be looking at parameters and doing something in a very elegant way that was too much work for a simple task in JavaScript. jQuery made JavaScript coding better but Knockout brings binding simplicity that we all needed from the start.

Next, we will create the markup for our example. We see the data-bind this time is connected to the checked value changing. The second input box is tied to the same ViewModel item, bringingSpouse. The second input stores the value entered into the ViewModel item, spouseName. When first loading the page it will not store anything because the input box will be disabled.

```
<p>
    Will you be bringing your spouse?
    <input type="checkbox" name="bringspouse" data-bind="checked:
    bringingSpouse" />
</p>
<p>
```

```
Your Spouse's Name:
<input type="text" data-bind="value: spouseName, enable:
bringingSpouse" />
</p>
```

This is the code to drive the automated logic. It just takes two observables; one to hold the value for the spouse's name and the other to handle true or false, to toggle the input box when the user has a spouse.

```
<script>
var vm = {
    bringingSpouse: ko.observable(false),
    spouseName: ko.observable("")
};
ko.applyBindings(vm);
</script>
```

Now, we can test our code to see how this works. It is as simple as clicking on the checkbox, following which the input box should become usable and ready for you to enter your spouse's name, if that applies to you, of course:

Will you be bringing your spouse? ✔
Your Spouse's Name:

Modifier keys

We are going to revisit our `enable.html` file and learn a little how to deal with some modified events. In our case, we will be looking at spotting the event when the *Shift* key is pressed. If *Shift* is pressed we will handle the event one way and if not, we will handle it another way. First, let's add a reset button to the screen with this HTML code:

```
<br/>
<button data-bind="event: {mouseover: reset }">RESET</button>
```

Now, we will add the highlighted code in the script section of the page:

```
var vm = {
    oneClass: ko.observable('putLeft'),
    twoClass: ko.observable('putLeft'),
    oneLeft: function() {
        this.oneClass('putLeft');
    },
    oneRight: function() {
        this.oneClass('putRight');
    },
    twoLeft: function() {
        this.twoClass('putLeft');
    },
    twoRight: function() {
        this.twoClass('putRight');
    },
    reset: function(data, event){
        if(event.shiftKey){
            alert("Don't hold the shift key!");
        } else {
            this.oneClass('putLeft');
            this.twoClass('putLeft');
        }
    }
};
```

When we hover the mouse over the new button with the *Shift* key pressed, it will pull up an alert box similar to this:

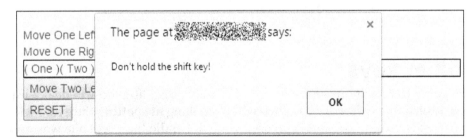

Default actions

By default, Knockout prevents the built-in standard browser events from taking place. If you want to let these events run, just bind a handler to the event that returns true.

Preventing bubbling

Another thing you may want to do is to prevent event bubbling. **Bubbling** means that an element on the web page, also called the DOM element, has a chain relationship with what we will call higher-level elements. After an item has had an opportunity to handle an event, the events are then passed up the chain to allow a higher element an opportunity to respond to the event.

In our mouseover example, there could have been an area of the page wrapping the button that also had a mouseover handler. If there was, after the button handled the event, the event would have been passed to the higher element to allow it to respond to the event as well.

Control is actually very simple. We only need to prevent the event by telling our button handler to return false. Of course, in a different scenario, for the event action which you don't want to go beyond, you would have set its handler return false value just like the button in our use case example we are discussing here.

The textInput binding

We have obviously done a number of bindings to textboxes already. Now, we are going to do something new with them. We are going to put a text input and a text area on the page together. Here is our HTML markup, where we will put in a new file called `text.html`:

```
<p>Title: <input data-bind="textInput: title" /></p>
<p>Post: <textarea data-bind="textInput: post" /></textarea></p>
<p>
<h2 data-bind="text: title"></h2>
<div data-bind="text: post"></div>
</p>
```

If we were using the value binding we would only get an update when the input element lost focus. Using the `textInput` binding let us have character by character feedback. Let's add our code so we can try it out:

```
<script>
function Blog() {
  this.title = ko.observable();
  this.post = ko.observable();
};
```

```
blog = new Blog();
ko.applyBindings( blog );
</script>
```

We see the page content updating character by character as we type but there is an issue. The text in the **Post** is coming into the page as text. There is a simple way to fix that. We just change the content target from text to html. Oh, and make sure you use small letters or you will have an issue. Now, run it again and it should look like this:

Dynamic focus

There are many opportunities to enhance user experience when doing dynamic AJAX style sites. Years ago, a website was a dead experience compared to the power you could add to a desktop application. Today, the more dynamic application is left up to the creative ability of the designers and developers on each platform. Changing the user interface to be more responsive creates a virtual relationship between the user and your page. Make use of the following steps to make your page dynamic:

1. The first thing we will do is change the `data-bind` attribute on the title of the text input. By adding a comma we can have more than one data binding on an element. We will add the `hasFocus` binder to the input, and target the event to call the handler that we will name `lookAtTitleBox`. Our input box should now look like this in the code:

```
<input data-bind="textInput: title, hasFocus:
  lookAtTitleBox" />
```

2. Next, we will add a button after this input box to show the ability to dynamically control the focus from code. This means we need to tie an event handler, our function, to the click event of the button. Then, we will let the code take care of passing control back to the title input box. Add this markup right after our title input box:

```
<button data-bind="click: focusTitle">Focus On
  Title</button>
```

3. Now, we will need to add our output text for the View to be displayed when the title input has the focus:

```
<span data-bind="visible:lookAtTitleBox">( Enter A Good
  Title )</span>
```

4. The last thing we need to do is modify our ViewModel to make our form more interactive. We will add two items: an observable attribute on our ViewModel and a method to be called by our View element:

```
this.lookAtTitleBox = ko.observable(false);
this.focusTitle = function(){
  this.lookAtTitleBox(true);
};
```

When the page is reloaded, our title field has the focus, by default. Click inside **Post** to remove the focus from the title element. You should see the focus text after the button is visible and when the title element has focus. Now, when the title element does not have focus, click on the **Focus On Title** button. You will see through Knockout that we are able to designate the focus of an element by toggling a variable in the ViewModel. This is another example of what makes ViewModels in MVVM oriented applications powerful. Here is the output we get when the page is reloaded:

Our complete code for this logic should look like the following:

```
<!-- Here is the markup code-->
<br/>
<p>Title: <input data-bind="textInput: title, hasFocus:
  lookAtTitleBox" />
<button data-bind="click: focusTitle">Focus On Title</button>
<span data-bind="visible:lookAtTitleBox">
( Enter A Good Title )
</span>
</p>
<p>Post: <textarea data-bind="textInput: post" /></textarea></p>
<p>
<h2 data-bind="text: title"></h2>
<div data-bind="html: post"></div>
</p>

// Here is the script code
<script>
function Blog() {
  this.title = ko.observable();
  this.post = ko.observable();
  this.lookAtTitleBox = ko.observable(false);
  this.focusTitle = function(){
    this.lookAtTitleBox(true);
  };
};
blog = new Blog();
ko.applyBindings( blog );
</script>
```

Take a moment and look at the elegant simplicity of this code. This is why many Knockout coders feel like what jQuery did for JavaScript, Knockout does as much to enhance the design and development experience.

Well, that is not good enough. If the goal is improved user experience why don't we copy this file, text.html, as text3.html and create a Web 3.0 level experience? We will just show all the code at once and talk through it. We will be creating the click-to-edit experience here:

```
<p>
  <span data-bind="click:editTitle">Title</span>:
  <input data-bind="visible: showTitleEditor, textInput: title,
  hasFocus:showTitleEditor" />
  <span data-bind="visible: !showTitleEditor(), html:title, click:
  editTitle"></span>
```

```
</p>
<p>
  <span data-bind="click:editPost">Post</span>:
  <textarea data-bind="visible: showPostEditor, textInput: post,
  hasFocus:showPostEditor" /></textarea>
  <span data-bind="visible: !showPostEditor(), html:post, click:
  editPost"></span>
</p>
```

What we have done is put the input element for the title with a span that displays the contents of the title value. You will notice they both have the same item starting the data-bind attribute. The order is not important as far as the code is stable; this is just the order we happen to code in. The visible item in the text has parentheses because the ! (not) symbol means we have entered JavaScript code into the attribute value. Whenever we do that we need to enter parentheses for it to function correctly.

We also have added a click event handler to the label and the title content. The reason we have added the label is that there will be times when you may have a page load without the title prepopulated. This was just an example to show that you still have access to calling the edit box by clicking on the title. When the page loads it will look like this at first (remember to complete the ViewModel before so that it will work correctly):

Title: Web 3.0

Post: Here is my **Web 3.0** content!

We want the same functionality for the **Post** box so you can see our code in the markup is identical, except it is a textArea field for the post versus the title. Now, let's look at our ViewModel code:

```
<script>
function Blog() {
  this.title = ko.observable('Web 3.0');
  this.showTitleEditor = ko.observable(false);
  this.editTitle = function(){
    this.showTitleEditor(true);
  };

  this.post = ko.observable('Here is my <strong>Web 3.0</strong>
  content!');
```

```
    this.showPostEditor = ko.observable(false);
    this.editPost = function(){
      this.showPostEditor(true);
    };
  };
blog = new Blog();
ko.applyBindings( blog );
</script>
```

We see that our values for the title and the visibility of the title editor are simple observable attributes on our ViewModel. The only thing we need the `editTitle` event handler to do is toggle the visible state of the title input box to true. Knockout will set the visibility of our View and edit elements correctly for us with hardly any code. We did the same thing for the post element. Now, when we click either on the title content or the title label, we will see the edit box for the title display as follows:

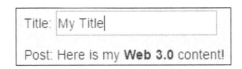

Radio and checkbox binding

Radio and checkbox handling in forms can be a pain. This is another area where Knockout just makes things simple. Our example will start by creating a file named `radio.html` this time. Let's start with the markup for our checkbox:

```
<h2>Checkbox</h2>
<p>
  Colors (<span data-bind="text: colors"></span>)<br/>
  <input type="checkbox" value="red" data-bind="checked: colors"
  /> Red<br/>
  <input type="checkbox" value="green" data-bind="checked: colors"
  /> Green<br/>
  <input type="checkbox" value="blue" data-bind="checked: colors"
  /> Blue<br/>
  <input type="checkbox" value="yellow" data-bind="checked:
  colors" /> Yellow<br/>
  <input type="checkbox" value="purple" data-bind="checked:
  colors" /> Purple<br/>
</p>
```

Now, add this code in a `script` tag on the bottom of the page, as we have done for the other pages. We will need an array to hold the contents of the selected items and that is basically all we need in our ViewModel for this functionality:

```
function VM() {
   this.colors = ko.observableArray([]);
};
vm = new VM();
ko.applyBindings( vm );
```

By binding the checked handler in the `data-bind` attributes, we will see that the `colors` attribute is automatically populated. The `colors` attribute in the `span` tag will show all of the currently selected checkbox elements. You might even try clicking earlier items on and off and you will see it always puts the last selected item at the end of the list:

The markup for a radio button is very similar. We are going to create our code the same way to show the difference in function between a radio button collection and a checkbox collection of elements, as follows:

```
<h2>Radio</h2>
<p>
   Shapes (<span data-bind="text: shapes"></span>)<br/>
```

```
<input type="radio" value="square" data-bind="checked: shapes"
/>Square<br/>
<input type="radio" value="round" data-bind="checked: shapes"
/>Round<br/>
<input type="radio" value="triangle" data-bind="checked: shapes"
/>Triangle<br/>
<input type="radio" value="rectangle" data-bind="checked:
shapes" />Rectangle<br/>
<input type="radio" value="oval" data-bind="checked: shapes"
/>Oval<br/>
</p>
```

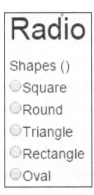

All we need to is just add this single line of code in `function VM()`:

```
this.shapes = ko.observableArray([]);
```

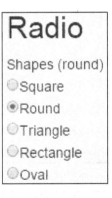

With the radio button it does not matter how many items are clicked, as radio buttons always limit themselves to a single item being selected. In common HTML, we would have needed to put a name on each of the radio buttons to make sure the DOM knew how to achieve this functionality. In this example, we can plainly see again that Knockout is taking care of business for us.

Enhanced event integration

The radio and checkbox binding, which we explained earlier, is useful and many seasoned developers likely think that HTML coding is far too heavy with the manual entering of all the details of colors or shapes right in the markup or the View part of the document. This type of thing is the best practice to place in a data collection of some sort. And this is exactly what we will do with the another set of checkboxes that we will label as **Foods**.

In this example, we will add an attribute to our ViewModel called `foodItems`. We will also go another step forward and set some preselected values in a variable called `foods`. You will notice that our `foodItems` attribute has a structured collection with two nested items: `item` and `itemDisplay`. Make sure your preselected items are using the `item` value. If you put in `Milk` instead of `milk` you will be confused about why it did not appear to work correctly. Items have to have a 100 percent match so lower case and upper case make all the difference here. Add the following code in `function VM()`:

```
this.foodItems = ko.observableArray([
  { item: 'bread', itemDisplay: 'Bread' },
  { item: 'milk', itemDisplay: 'Milk' },
  { item: 'eggs', itemDisplay: 'Eggs' }
]);
this.foods = ko.observableArray(['bread', 'eggs'"]);
```

Now, we can add in another set of checkboxes for the foods in the View section of our code. We will also be using the foreach binding in this set. Here, we can pass a JSON style structure to allow us to create an alias of "food" for our internal `$data` item. Each item inside `foreach` is designated as `$data`. Adding the as key allows us to set an alias for the `$data` as food. We show both approaches in use here by using `$data.item` and by using `food.itemDisplay` for the more dynamic example. Here is the code to add in the markup:

```
<h2>Checkbox</h2>
<p>
  Foods (<span data-bind="text: foods"></span>)<br/>
<div data-bind="foreach: {data:foodItems, as: 'food'}">
```

```
  <input type="checkbox" data-bind="checkedValue: $data.item, checked:
$root.foods" />
  <span data-bind="text: food.itemDisplay"></span><br/>
</div>
</p>
```

This is our complete code, in case it would help you to see all in one place. Knockout again has shown a simpler and powerful advantage to the way it works.

```
function VM() {
  this.colors = ko.observableArray([]);
  this.shapes = ko.observableArray([]);
  this.foodItems = ko.observableArray([
    { item: 'bread', itemDisplay: 'Bread' },
    { item: 'milk', itemDisplay: 'Milk' },
    { item: 'eggs', itemDisplay: 'Eggs' }
  ]);
  this.foods = ko.observableArray(["bread","eggs"]);
};
vm = new VM();
ko.applyBindings( vm );
```

Select binding

Our first example of using Knockout with a `select` element will be for single item selection. This is the markup where we will put `colors` into the options:

```
<p>
  Colors: ( <span data-bind="text: colors"></span> )
  <br/>
  <select data-bind="options: colorOptions,
              value: colors,
              optionsCaption: 'Choose a color'"></select>
</p>
```

In our code we will be doing one more special thing at this time. After we create the ViewModel we will modify one of its attributes and add another color to the colorOptions array using the push function, common to JavaScript. This means that some parts of JavaScript are great already and we should continue to use them. Here is the script code:

```
<script>
function MyModel(){
   this.colorOptions = ko.observableArray(['Red','Green','Blue','Yello
w','Green']);
   this.colors = ko.observableArray();
};
myModel = new MyModel();
ko.applyBindings( myModel );
myModel.colorOptions.push('Orange');
</script>
```

```
Colors: ( Orange )
Orange          ▼
```

If we select the last added item, **Orange**, we will see the selector and the display span both showing the value as in the preceding screenshot. Using the code you can set the value of the ViewModel color attribute and it will automatically set the select box to the matching value. You should try it from the browser developer tools console. Don't forget to match the case of the value.

Now, we will use a multi-select element. We don't need the options caption in this case. What we do need is to change the values of the data-bind handler to the selectedOptions handler. This allows us to capture multiple items. Just remember that a value is singular and selected options are plural. I am not saying that we always have to think of singular and plural, but we do in this case. Add the following code to the markup:

```
<p>
   Shapes: ( <span data-bind="text: shapes"></span> )
   <br/>
   <select size="3" multiple="true"
     data-bind="options: shapeOptions,
        selectedOptions: shapes"></select>
</p>
```

Now, it's time to add in a little bit of code to work with the new select element. There is no pragmatic difference between the data coding of a single select and the multi-select element in the ViewModel.

```
this.shapeOptions =
    ko.observableArray(['Square','Circle','Triangle','Rectangle',
    'Oval']);
this.shapes = ko.observableArray();
```

As you can see in the following screenshot, this works really well by allowing us to select multiple elements:

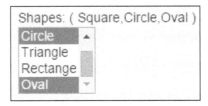

Selecting elements with the object collections

Sometimes our data comes with the value and the displayed item representing the value as two different items. Here is an example of how to code when this is the case:

```
<p>
   Budget:
   <br/>
   <select data-bind="options: budgets,
         optionsText: 'budgetName',
         value: budget,
         optionsCaption: 'Pick...'"></select>
</p>
<div>
   You have chosen a
   '<span data-bind="text: budget() ? budget().budgetType :
   'undeclared'"></span>'
   budget type.
</div>
```

And in the `script` tag, inside `MyModel()`, add the following line of code:

```
this.budget = ko.observable();
```

Notice `optionsText` is not a variable but is the value of the structure element inside the collection item. We are using an individual result here so we use the value handler to hold the results. If it were multiple selections, we would use the `selectedOptions` binding. Here is what the initial display will look like after our code is added. Notice that the type is set to `undeclared`:

Also take note of the logic inside our text binding. If there is no item selected, the budget item will be a null item. This works in JavaScript as a false result. It will then display the contents of the item after the colon. Otherwise it returns the results of the item before the colon. In that case we will return the structure element from the budget item for the type, which you will see in our script; we coded it as `budgetType`. Let's take a look at the `script` code now:

```
var Budget = function(name, type){
    this.budgetName = name;
    this.budgetType = type;
};
```

The code segment above will come before we declare the structure of our ViewModel. We will use it to declare the items within our budget collection as follows. We use a simple observable versus an observableArray because we are only returning a single item. It is a structured item with nested attributes but it is a single item at that level and thus, this is the correct logic:

```
this.budgets = ko.observableArray([
    new Budget('Electric','expense'),
    new Budget('Bob Pay','income'),
    new Budget('Betty Pay','income'),
    new Budget('Taxes','expense'),
    new Budget('Gas','expense'),
    new Budget('Rental House','income'),
    new Budget('House Payment','expense')
]);
this.budget = ko.observable();
```

Now, let's look at the results once we select an item. If we select the **Rental House** item we see that the budget type changes to **income**. This makes for nice dynamic interaction with far less manual coding of our automated systems.

Listing the management Knockout style

Now we can take our budget system just a little further. We will make a list editor that will let us add, delete, and sort our list. While most of what we have done so far has been very simple, this one is going to be different. This example is going to be simplified. It does a lot more so it will take a little more. Yet, through the power of Knockout, we will see that simplicity is still intact:

```html
<p>
  <form data-bind="submit:addBudget">
  Budget Editor:
  <hr/>
  Budget:
  <input data-bind="value: newName, valueUpdate: 'afterkeydown'"
  /><br/>
  Type:
  <select data-bind="options: budgetTypes,
              value: budgetType"></select><br/>
  <button type="submit" data-bind="enable: newName().length">Add
  Budget</button>
  </form>
</p>
```

In our first section of code we use something that we have not used so far. We use a form tag. Normally forms are not used when coding with Knockout. So why the change in this example? The change is because we are going to use the submit function of the form to act as our trigger to add the new budget items to our budget. This is done with the addBudget handler in our code. Here is our script code:

```javascript
this.newName = ko.observable("");
this.budgetTypes = ko.observableArray(['income','expense']);
this.budgetType = ko.observable();
this.selectedBudgets = ko.observableArray([]);
this.addBudget = function(){
  var myBudget = new Budget(this.newName(),this.budgetType());
  if((this.newName() != "")
      && (this.budgets.indexOf(myBudget) < 0) ) {
    this.budgets.push(myBudget);
  }
  this.newName("");
};
this.dropBudget = function(){
  this.budgets.removeAll(this.selectedBudgets());
};
```

```
this.sortBudgets = function(){
  this.budgets.sort(bCompare);
};
```

Most of the rest of the code looks familiar. The only part that might be new for some is the sorting of budgets. We do this using the standard JavaScript style sorting and a custom function we created outside the ViewModel. The custom function is the bCompare function. Here is the code for that:

```
var bCompare = function(left,right){
  if(left.budgetName < right.budgetName) {
    return -1;
  }
  if(left.budgetName > right.budgetName) {
    return 1;
  }
  return 0;
};
```

This is a simple compare function used by JavaScript to interact with the natural flow to make sure that all the items are in order. Again, we see that the code behind this edit form is simple enough. Let's take a look at the list editor we are building. We did not make it fancy but we are certainly building some sweet functionality into it:

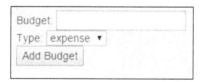

There is a little more special markup in the View side of the code to make sure things are bound correctly, shown as follows:

```
<p>
  <select size="5" multiple="true"
      data-bind="options: budgets,
              optionsText: 'budgetName',
              selectedOptions: selectedBudgets"></select>
</p>
<p>
  <button data-bind="click: dropBudget">Drop Budget</button>
  <button data-bind="click: sortBudgets">Sort Budgets</button>
</p>
```

Now, if you are looking at the code you may be wondering what is special about the code. It's just Knockout making things simple and powerful. This is all it takes to get the job done. Oh, did you figure out that I am pretty impressed with Knockout? I am. Knockout is what makes it special because it is doing so much for us so that we can concentrate on the programming goals instead of how to achieve them. Here is a screenshot after we add **Entertainment** as an expense, sort the list, and delete **Gas** from it:

The uniqueName binding

IE6 does not allow radio buttons to be checked if they don't have a name attribute. Most of the time this is irrelevant because your radio button elements will have the name attributes to put them into mutually-exclusive groups. However, if you didn't add a name attribute because it's unnecessary in your case, Knockout will internally use uniqueName on those elements to ensure they can be checked. Hopefully, none of us will have to use IE6 but just in case, add the uniqueName handler to the data-bind attribute, something like this if needed:

```
<input data-bind="value: newName, uniqueName: true" />
```

Grid forms

Now we will take our budget form just one step further. We will combine a number of the features we have been learning to this point into an editable grid. We will wrap the grid in a form this time also, but you will see in the code a dual option for how you use the form. Create a file called grid.html for this example. Enter the following in the markup:

```
<form action='/serverTargetHandlerHere'>
  <p>You have asked for <span data-bind='text: budget().
length'> </span> budget item(s)</p>
```

```
<table data-bind='visible: budget().length > 0'>
  <thead>
    <tr>
      <th>Budget</th>
      <th>Amount</th>
      <th/>
    </tr>
  </thead>
  <tbody data-bind='foreach: budget'>
    <tr>
      <td><input data-bind='value: name, uniqueName: true'
/></td>
      <td><input data-bind='value: amount, uniqueName: true'
/></td>
      <td><a href='#' data-bind='click:
$root.removeBudget'>Delete</a></td>
    </tr>
  </tbody>
</table>
<button data-bind='click: addBudget'>Add Budget</button>
<button data-bind='enable: budget().length > 0,click: save'
type''='submit'>Submit</button>
</form>
```

If you want to use Knockout just as an automated editor and still submit the form, you could fill in the details on the action attribute of the form and still submit it in the old-school approach. This might be useful if you are working with an older system and your business logic is still form-submission based. This will also allow you to enter the realm of Knockout more gradually. It could also allow you to test out the functionality without having to totally rewrite your systems during testing this way.

Notice we are using the foreach markup binding to manage a row in our grid for every data row on the model of our data. The ViewModel smartly keeps all of this tied together and up to date. We have also added in the uniqueName logic that one would add into an application that needs to support IE6. Now let's look at the script code:

```
var BudgetModel = function(budget) {
    var self = this;
    self.budget = ko.observableArray(budget);
    self.addBudget = function() {
        self.budget.push({
            name: "",
            amount: ""
```

```
            });
        };
        self.removeBudget = function(budget) {
            self.budget.remove(budget);
        };
        self.save = function(form) {
            alert("Could now transmit to server: " +
      ko.utils.stringifyJson(self.budget));
            // To actually transmit to server as a regular form post,
      write this: ko.utils.postJson($("form")[0], self.budget);
        };
    };
    var budget = new BudgetModel([
        { name: "Food", amount: "560.00"},
        { name: "Utilities", amount: "180.00"},
        { name: "Rent", amount: "620.00"},
        { name: "Insurance", amount: "80.00"}
    ]);
    ko.applyBindings( budget );
```

We created a standard ViewModel named BudgetModel in this example. Once again, we are using the JavaScript array push method to stack another budget item in our array collection. We also have handlers for removing a budget item. If we look back at our markup you will see it uses the scope-based variable $root.removeBudget. The rows are added using the foreach functionality so Knockout once again does the heavy lifting for us and it will know which row you are trying to delete. Don't get stressed out trying to figure it out. Think of it like a smartphone. You don't need to know how it works. What you need to know is how to use it.

The save method handler is set to show the results in an alert box. You could have easily used jQuery AJAX to send these results back to a server for persistent data storage. You will also see there is, as stated previously, the ability to just send it as a form. The choice is there for you to pick the one that best suits your needs. Here is the screenshot for the previous code:

You have asked for 3 budget item(s)		
Budget	**Amount**	
Food	560.00	Delete
Rent	620.00	Delete
Clothing	40.00	Delete
Add Budget	Submit	

Now play around with this example. Add some rows. Delete some rows. Click **Submit** with data and you will see the results in an alert box. Click it without any rows and you will see it is smart enough to just ignore the user trying to submit nothing.

Summary

When working with forms and grids, and keeping the data up to date, anytime you touch it, anywhere, is what Knockout has been about from the start. I hope you are enjoying coding web forms with the simple but powerful advances this technology offers. It makes focusing on business logic much easier with less code.

In the next chapter, we will learn to integrate data management in Knockout using JSON and mapping.

4
Coding – AJAX, Binding Properties, Mapping, and Utilities

There is an aspect of Knockout that takes repeated tasks out of the way. There is also the reality that we never expect it to do 100 percent of our work. It also makes sense that we do not have Knockout doing so much as it is not good at its core strengths. Here, we will learn how to extend our reach into Knockout and how to connect to the world outside Knockout and do even more. This chapter will focus on:

- Working with JSON
- Mapping versus manual ViewModels
- Working with AJAX requests
- Unmapping your data
- Managed mapping
- Utility functions

In this chapter, we will be learning about some of the commonly used aspects of Knockout—working with JSON and the mapping plugin. These two are simple and powerful pivots where we will extend rapid application development with Knockout.

JSON done Knockout style

JSON is the famous data packaging standard that seems to have taken over the Internet. At one time there was XML; RoR has its own packaging standard; and even Adobe had perhaps the best performing way to package and deliver data between the client and the server called **Action Message Format (AMF)**. The overall winner seems to be JSON because it is simple and based on the most common development platform of all: JavaScript. If you would like more information about JSON you can visit http://json.org.

To serve our purpose, let's create a file called, json.html. The first thing we will do is convert a ViewModel to JSON. Most modern browsers have a function called JSON.stringify but that is not how we do it in Knockout. There are two methods included in Knockout:

- ko.toJS
- ko.toJSON

The first method, ko.toJS, will clone the Knockout data into a plain copy that contains no Knockout-related hints or information. The second method, ko.toJSON, will perform the ko.toJS action and then convert it into a serialized JSON string according to the JSON standard. If you are using older browsers such as IE7 or older, you will need to get a copy of the json2.js file, available at https://github.com/douglascrockford/JSON-js/blob/master/json2.js.

Now enter the following code into your file:

```
<script>
function VM() {
  this.colors = ko.observableArray([]);
  this.shapes = ko.observableArray([]);
  this.foodItems = ko.observableArray([
    { item: 'bread', itemDisplay: 'Bread' },
    { item: 'milk', itemDisplay: 'Milk' },
    { item: 'eggs', itemDisplay: 'Eggs' }
  ]);
  this.foods = ko.observableArray(["bread","eggs"]);
};
vm = new VM();
ko.applyBindings( vm );
</script>
```

Now we will look at our structure stored in the ViewModel. We will be using Chrome as our browser but you can use any browser with development tools that support the console command. Here is the result we got by dumping our ViewModel. Type `console.log(vm)` in the console to get the results stored in vm:

```
> console.log( vm )
  ▶ VM {colors: function, shapes: function, foodItems: function, foods: function}
  undefined
```

It is plainly visible that while a full exposure of our ViewModel is there, packaged in functions. You will get used to ignoring the `undefined` item, when dumping stuff into the console. If you get the results expected then don't get distracted by that item.

This is where we use the two commands, which are `ko.toJS` and `ko.toJSON`. Let's start by dumping the ViewModel to the console using the structure. Type `console.log( ko.toJS(vm) )` in the console:

```
> console.log( ko.toJS(vm) )
  ▼ Object {colors: Array[0], shapes: Array[0], foodItems: Array[3], foods: Array[2]} ▦
    ▶ colors: Array[0]
    ▼ foodItems: Array[3]
      ▼ 0: Object
          item: "bread"
          itemDisplay: "Bread"
        ▶ __proto__: Object
      ▶ 1: Object
      ▶ 2: Object
        length: 3
      ▶ __proto__: Array[0]
    ▶ foods: Array[2]
    ▶ shapes: Array[0]
    ▶ __proto__: Object
  undefined
```

Here, we see `console.log` versus dump. This is great, but if we wanted to send this out to an external source or store it using modern browser storage technology we would still want to package it as a JSON string in most cases. This can be achieved using the helper `ko.toJSON` method, which is what we will be doing next. You will see this time our data has been placed in the middle of special characters. This is the JSON formatting, as shown in the following screenshot:

```
> console.log( ko.toJSON(vm) )
  {"colors":[],"shapes":[],"foodItems":[{"item":"bread","itemDisplay":"Bread"},
  {"item":"milk","itemDisplay":"Milk"},{"item":"eggs","itemDisplay":"Eggs"}],"foods":
  ["bread","eggs"]}
  undefined
```

Now, we will create `json2.html` to pull our JSON data into our app. We will need to copy and paste the JSON into our app but we will be doing that from a separate file in the same directory as the HTML file. Name that file `json2.txt` for this example. Certainly, on a live site don't store sensitive data in a text file. In the `json2.txt` file copy the console output you got in the preceding example. This is your JSON data and it should look like this:

```
{"colors":[],"shapes":[],"foodItems":[{"item":"bread","itemDisplay":"B
read"},{"item":"milk","itemDisplay":"Milk"},{"item":"eggs","itemDispla
y":"Eggs"}],"foods":["bread","eggs"]}
```

While this might look good, we have an issue. JSON doesn't stand on its own feet. It needs to be inside a variable to be managed. We will change it as follows. We will use the variable, `myJSON`. We also need to surround the text in quotes. Since the JSON tends to use double quotes internally, the traditional way to handle this is to use a single quote before the data string and a single quote at the end, as shown in the following code:

```
myJSON =
    '{"colors":[],"shapes":[],"foodItems":[{"item":"bread",
    "itemDisplay":"Bread"},{"item":"milk","itemDisplay":"Milk"},
    {"item":"eggs","itemDisplay":"Eggs"}],"foods":["bread","eggs"]}';
```

The following code is used for our `json2.html` file. We will use the `script` command to pull the external data into the page. It is also common for people to name such a static file `json2.json`. We are using the `.text` extension to make a point that JSON is just a text file here:

```
<script src="json2.txt"></script>
<script>
function VM() {
   this.colors = ko.observableArray([]);
   this.shapes = ko.observableArray([]);
   this.foodItems = ko.observableArray([]);
   this.foods = ko.observableArray([]);
};
vm = new VM();
ko.applyBindings( vm );
myData = JSON.parse(myJSON);
vm.foodItems(myData.foodItems);
vm.foods(myData.foods);
</script>
```

We start out our ViewModel this time with structure but absolutely no data. After binding the ViewModel to our data model, we convert our string of JSON data into a standard JavaScript structure. We then use the standard JavaScript to pass the arrays into the `foodItems` and the `foods` attributes of our ViewModel. While that is neat, it doesn't feel like we actually did something of value. Let's add some View code onto the page above the `script` section, as follows. This is the same code we used in the previous chapter:

```
Foods (<span data-bind="text: foods"></span>)<br/>
<div data-bind="foreach: {data:foodItems, as: 'food'}">
  <input type="checkbox" data-bind="checkedValue:$data.item,
  checked: $root.foods" />
  <span data-bind="text: food.itemDisplay"></span><br/>
</div>
```

What we see is a web page that pulls the external data in and automatically populates the View for us based on that data:

Mapping – first look

We have been creating manual maps of our ViewModel so far in this book. With smaller datasets this can be practical and productive. As our datasets get larger along with the need to update the data, this will become a chore that has an alternative, enjoyed by a great number of Knockout developers. This is done through a mapping plugin. Knockout is a jQuery-based library in more than one way. It is possible to build and use libraries, called plugins, for Knockout also. The most famous library is the mapping library. I have included a copy of it in the downloaded files for this book. We will be looking again at the preceding code for our example but moving it this time using the mapping plugin.

We will create a file called `mapping.html` for our code this time. We will need to include one more JavaScript file right after the Knockout call for our mapping plugin. You can find these files in the working examples folder in the ZIP download. This, in our case, should look like this:

```
<script src="json2.txt"></script>
<script src="data.js"></script>
```

Create both of those files if you wish, but we suggest just copying them from the done folder in this chapter and making sure they are in the same folder as the mapping.html file.

Connecting with AJAX remotely

Using a script tag to load data is definitely not very sophisticated. We are going to improve this by creating the example again, but this time using jQuery to make our AJAX request. We will put this code in a file named ajax.html. We will use the same HTML code as before, but we will add a button to the form using the following lines of code:

```
Foods (<span data-bind="text: foods"></span>)
<button data-bind="click: pullData">Pull Data</button><br/>
<div data-bind="foreach: {data:foodItems, as: 'food'}">
  <input type="checkbox" data-bind="checkedValue:$data.item,
  checked: $root.foods" />
  <span data-bind="text: food.itemDisplay"></span><br/>
</div>
```

The pullData request will be a method/function that we add to our ViewModel. It will be used, at this time, to pull the data from the server and update the View in our browser. Here is the script section of code we will use for this example:

```
<script>
function VM() {
  var self = this;
  self.foodItems = ko.observableArray([]);
  self.foods = ko.observableArray([]);
  self.pullData = function(){
    var reqAJAX = "data.json";
    jQuery.getJSON(reqAJAX).done(function(data){
      self.foodItems(data.foodItems);
      self.foods(data.foods);
    });
  };
};
vm = new VM();
ko.applyBindings( vm );
</script>
```

Please note that I am going to try to get you into the habit of using – this is a phrase I made up and like – "selfish coding". Because there is a risk of interaction with our code having the `this` value, debugging "this" issue is not fun. We have learned to use the `self` alias to make sure this does not become an issue. The `.done()` function is a chained command in jQuery to handle the completion of a good request to the server. See the jQuery documents for more handlers; you can use those docs to make your code even more fully responsive.

We have created a function/method called `pullData`. Inside the data we will use a `jQuery.getJSON` request to pull our data back from the server. We have copied the JSON structure to a file called `data.json` this time. Make sure you do not assign this to a variable; you only want the structure of the JSON as follows:

```
{"colors":[],"shapes":[],"foodItems":[{"item":"bread","itemDisplay":"B
read"},{"item":"milk","itemDisplay":"Milk"},{"item":"eggs","itemDispla
y":"Eggs"}],"foods":["bread","eggs"]}
```

Now let's look at our initial screen when we load the page. Here is what you should get:

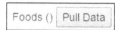

When we click the **Pull Data** button we will see the results automatically update to the following view:

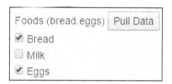

This is already much better coding than a pure JavaScript experience for many developers. Yet, what if this form had 40 elements on the page? It would be a big block of code to set the ViewModel up for that much binding. We just learned about mapping; so what if we included the mapping plugin and reworked our code? Take a look at the following piece of code:

```
<script>
var reqAJAX = "data.json";
vm = {};
jQuery.getJSON(reqAJAX).done(function(data){
    vm = ko.mapping.fromJS(data);
    vm.pullData = function(){
```

```
      reqAJAX = "data2.json";
      jQuery.getJSON(reqAJAX).done(function(data){
         ko.mapping.fromJS(data,vm);
      });
   };
   ko.applyBindings( vm );
});
</script>
```

We can see a few changes in our approach. We could have just put the filename into the getJSON request, but we passed it in as a variable just as a matter of how we like to code. We also created the vm variable to hold our ViewModel.

The AJAX has been moved outside the ViewModel while the ViewModel declaration has been moved inside the AJAX. It is inside out compared to our last example. The difference is that we see the data populate our View immediately as the page loads. We have also changed the functionality of our pullData function. Now, it will be used to make a second call to the server. Normally, we would not reset this source file as it would be a typical AJAX request to see whether anything was updated. Since we are not coding for a dynamic server we will just show an imitation of that scenario here by changing the name of the source for our AJAX request.

Now, when doing mapping we have to declare the mapping features before we use the applyBindings method. This gives us the same results as manually creating each individual binding. Again, for a simple form like this the gain is not so obvious. When we get to larger, more complex pages, the gain is amazing. Oh, also note that when we run additional calls to the server we will be updating the data. We need to pass in the ViewModel variable after our data as we map an update.

Now, we will take another look at what we get by running our code with a little more progressive AJAX. The first load looks like the pulled data from our last example:

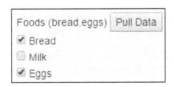

We created an additional item; so when we load the update it will be obvious. The item is **Ice Cream**. We also preselected this item. Here is our JSON data structure for the second load:

```
{"colors":[],"shapes":[],"foodItems":[{"item":"bread","itemDisplay":"B
read"},{"item":"milk","itemDisplay":"Milk"},{"item":"eggs","itemDispla
y":"Eggs"},{"item":"icecream","itemDisplay":"Ice Cream"}],"foods":["b
read","eggs"]}
```

When we push the button now to pull the update this is what we should see:

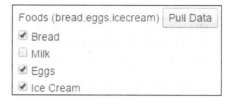

Unmapping your data

This is coming along good but there is something we are going to need for most AJAX-based web applications. We are going to need to store the data back on the server. Pulling the data to the browser will not be enough. We will require the ability to push the data back to the server as well. Once again, we will be using jQuery for this function. Of course, we will show the code to do this but we will approach it differently because different readers will be using different backends such as ASP.NET, ColdFusion, Node.js, PHP, Python, Ruby, and others.

This time, just modify the code in the AJAX.html file unless, of course, you want to create a new file. We will be adding another button to our View to connect a push data method this time:

```
<button data-bind="click:pushData">Push Data</button>
```

We will also need to put a textbox at the end of our View code to see the data that is pulled out of our ViewModel. Create the textarea field to hold the results:

```
<textarea id="unmapped"></textarea>
```

We will need to add another method to our ViewModel now:

```
<script>
var reqAJAX = "data.json";
vm = {};
jQuery.getJSON(reqAJAX).done(function(data){
  vm = ko.mapping.fromJS(data);
  vm.pullData = function(){
    reqAJAX = "data2.json";
    jQuery.getJSON(reqAJAX).done(function(data){
      ko.mapping.fromJS(data,vm);
    });
  };
  vm.pushData = function(){
    // This next line is just to show unmapped data
```

```
    var myData = ko.toJSON(vm);
    jQuery('#unmapped').text(myData);
    /*
    jQuery.post(reqAJAX, myData ).done(function(data){
      // code here to reflect good request
      alert("Your food changes have been stored.");
    });
    */
  };
  ko.applyBindings( vm );
});
</script>
```

We saw the code that would be used to send a request back to the server. We are assuming in this example that our server was able to respond to the URL in the reqAJAX variable and handle data coming into the server. If not, all you would need to do is set that variable to the target that can take data. The data is being sent in this case in the POST form of data. This would be the same as a form using the POST method.

You should see all we did was add the ability to pull the results back out as a variable named myData. If we ran the code again, pulled data, and set the selections to just eggs and ice cream, we would be able to test the data being pushed back to the server. Notice we have the jQuery command to push the myData results to the textarea field. Here are the results we see:

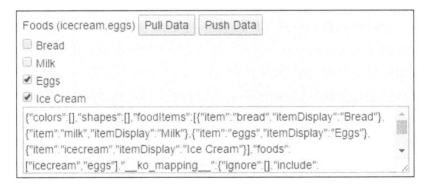

We have what seems to be an issue with extra data. We don't have to manage that but it is not hard to fix. The issue occurs because when data is mapped it creates extra details internally. These come back out when unmapping the data. You can leave that if you choose or you can fix it using the following code. We will write a console.log command that will dump the structure to the console. We also need to change myData to return the JavaScript structure.

If we look at our developer tools console for our browser we will see the following structure for our dump. Then we will use `JSON.stringify()` to make it ready for AJAX:

```
var myData = ko.toJS(vm);
console.log(myData);
delete myData.__ko_mapping__;
myData = JSON.stringify(myData);
jQuery('#unmapped').text(myData);
```

We see the change to the `myData` variable and the console log to manage the dump. The extra detail in the console log is part of the `__ko_mapping__` data structure. Using the JavaScript delete command, we can trim it right off our results. Some functions are showing, but when we use the `stringify` function, it does not pull them. Here is what we get now:

```
{"colors":[],"shapes":[],"foodItems":[{"item":"bread","itemDisplay":"B
read"},{"item":"milk","itemDisplay":"Milk"},{"item":"eggs","itemDispla
y":"Eggs"},{"item":"icecream","itemDisplay":"Ice Cream"}],"foods":["eg
gs","icecream"]}
```

Now we are doing meaningful AJAX interaction. You may want to send even less structure back to the server than we did here. There is the option of trimming even more data to keep things as compact as possible.

Oh, for a live app, *remember* to remove the console log and the `textarea` field. Don't say I taught you to leave those in a real world web page!

Merging mapped data

There are times you may want to pull data into your ViewModel from multiple sources. When doing this you can create a map for each source. If the source variables have the same name they will overwrite the existing variables. As long as the base variable is a different name it will merge them into the ViewModel. Do this as follows:

```
myViewModel = ko.mapping.fromJS(firstData, firstMap);
ko.mapping.fromJS(nextData, nextMap, myViewModel);
```

What you get is a combination of the `firstData` JavaScript structure, mapped with `firstMap`, combined with the `nextData` JavaScript structure, and with the `nextMap` mapping. If there are any duplicate base structures in `nextData`, they will override the same structures in the existing `firstData` JavaScript structure.

Mapping options

There are times when you are loading data into a page application that doesn't need to be changed. This is just static data and making it observable spends extra processor time and memory resources for no gain. When passing data into the mapping handler, you can set which items are mapped as observable items, using the following lines of code:

```
var data = {
  a: "a",
  b: [{ b1: "v1" }, { b2: "v2" }],
  c: true
};
var result = ko.mapping.fromJS(data, { observe: "a" });
var result2 = ko.mapping.fromJS(data, { observe: "a", copy: "b"
  }); //will be faster to map.
```

The results we get from the `result` and `result2` variables will be the same. Why? This is because when we declare the `observe` items the other items are assumed to be copied items. If a single item is passed in we can declare it outside an array, as we did with `a`. If multiple items are passed in we would declare them in an array, as `["a","c"]`. This would make both `a` and `c` observable items.

If we just wanted to declare an item to copy we would pass in the copy and that is the only item that would be directly copied. We also have the ability to ignore items from being copied in during the mapping using `ignore`, of course.

Utility functions

There are a number of functions in `ko.utils`. Let's start by looking at the special array methods in standard Knockout.

ko.utils.arrayFilter()

The `ko.utils.arrayFilter` function allows us to filter items in an array. We are going to run these as straight code examples. We will create a sample JSON file and load it via AJAX to keep the focus on learning the methods and not waste time creating an example code set. We will create a page called `utility.html` for these pieces of code and run the filtering code from there. Our markup for this example is here:

```
<h3>arrayFilter() : staff under 35</h3>
<ul data-bind="foreach: youngStaff">
  <li><span data-bind="text: age() + ' ' +
  firstName()"></span></li>
</ul>
```

Our `script` code is as follows. We will be adding more for each example as we go, but here are the basics for the utility examples:

```
<script>
var vm = {};
jQuery.getJSON('utility.json').done(function(data){
  vm = ko.mapping.fromJS( data );
  vm.youngStaff = ko.computed(function(){
    return ko.utils.arrayFilter(vm.arr(), function(item){
      if(item.age() < 35) { return true; }
      return false;
    });
  });
  ko.applyBindings(vm);
});
</script>
```

We set our mapping using the data and then we begin adding our custom features. These could be custom functions or computed values. Lastly, after adding all our customizations to the mapping we apply our bindings.

In our code sample we showed you how to use `arrayFilter`. The `arrayFilter` function will pass in the items one at a time and will include the ones in the result set in which we send out a true value to let it know that it should be included.

Here is the JSON we will use for our examples. We will show the whole dataset here. Note that the JSON is also in our `done` folder under the `utility.json` file if you do not want to type it in. Normally, I would suggest typing in these examples to strengthen your skills on the topic:

```
{"arr":[{"firstName":"James","lastName":"Donald","age":23,"phone":[]},
{"firstName":"Adam","lastName":"Thomas","age":46,"phone":[]},{"firstNa
me":"Michelle","lastName":"Ingram","age":32,"phone":[]},{"firstName":"
Edward","lastName":"Adams","age":63,"phone":[]},{"firstName":"Veronica
","lastName":"Wesson","age":54,"phone":[]},{"firstName":"Greg","lastNa
me":"Simons","age":46,"phone":[]}],"color_1":["red","green","blue","or
ange"],"color_2":["red","blue","orange","purple"]}
```

Also, we used the following dataset to create our JSON. We just called the JSON. `stringify` method on the dataset. Here is the code:

```
{
  arr : [
    { "firstName": "James", "lastName": "Donald", "age": 23,
    "phone": [] },
```

```
   { "firstName": "Adam", "lastName": "Thomas", "age": 46,
"phone": [] },
   { "firstName": "Michelle", "lastName": "Ingram", "age": 32,
"phone": [] },
   { "firstName": "Edward", "lastName": "Adams", "age": 63,
"phone": [] },
   { "firstName": "Veronica", "lastName": "Wesson", "age": 54,
"phone": [] },
   { "firstName": "Greg", "lastName": "Simons", "age": 46,
"phone": [] }
   ],
   color_1 : [ "red","green","blue","orange" ],
   color_2 : [ "red","blue","orange","purple" ]
}
```

We still need to include our jQuery, Knockout, and Knockout mapping JavaScript files. When you get all these pulled together with the preceding code, this is what you should see in your browser:

arrayFilter() : staff under 35

- 23 James
- 32 Michelle

We see that our filtered results only return two of the six items. This is because only two of them were less than 35. What is even more fun is that this data is dynamically wired into the View model. If the arrays change by adding or removing items the screen will update automatically. This is just not wired into jQuery so it's a great addition. Also, if a value within an array item changes, say one of the ages, then the filter here will automatically know to add, remove, or leave the item in the view list.

ko.utils.arrayFirst()

The `ko.utils.arrayFirst` method will pass items into the function to be searched until a match is found or declared. It will only return one item from the array. Here is the View code to add for this example:

```
<h3>arrayFirst() : first found over 45</h3>
( <span data-bind="text: firstRetire().age()"></span> )
```

Here is the logic to add to understand our `arrayFirst` utility command. Add it before the binding is set in our script:

```
vm.firstRetire = ko.computed(function(){
  return ko.utils.arrayFirst(vm.arr(), function(item){
```

```
    if(item.age() > 45) return true;
    return false;
  });
}); // arrayFirst
```

Like the last utility method, the results are triggered by the true value coming back out. The difference in this example is that the first true value will be the only one ever returned. Here is a screenshot of our results:

arrayFirst() : first found over 45

(46)

ko.utils.arrayMap()

The `ko.utils.arrayMap` method allows creation of a flattened array. What this means is that sometimes we have an array of structures and want just a particular item for the whole structure to be pulled back into a simple array. Here is the markup code:

```
<h3>arrayMap() : till retirment</h3>
<ul data-bind="foreach: tillRetire">
  <li><span data-bind="text: $data"></span></li>
</ul>
```

Here is the script code we need to add for this example. We will not return true or false style results this time. We will return a value that will, in this case, create a simple value array:

```
vm.tillRetire = ko.computed(function(){
  return ko.utils.arrayMap(vm.arr(),function(item){
    return 65 - item.age() + ' years till retirement.';
  })
}); // arrayMap()
```

This is the screen result you will see with our dataset:

arrayMap() : till retirment

- 42 years till retirement.
- 19 years till retirement.
- 33 years till retirement.
- 2 years till retirement.
- 11 years till retirement.
- 19 years till retirement.

It is possible to actually modify the structure that is being passed into the process by modifying the item. This is because normally, structures and arrays are passed in by setting a reference to the source structure in memory. This means even though the name item is what is coming in, the item points to the original structure in the ViewModel. Here is another method we could have used if we wanted to modify the original structure within the ViewModel:

```
vm.tillRetire2 = ko.computed(function(){
  ko.utils.arrayMap(vm.arr(),function(item){
    item.yearsLeft = 65 - item.age() + ' years till retirement.';
  })
}); // arrayMap()
```

The results would be a value nested within the ViewModel array collection, but the value would not be observed or computed. This means while it may work, it will not work with all the features of Knockout. So it should be tested carefully before trying this. If in doubt, avoid this approach to avoid unplanned features. Oh, you could also delete item fields, so beware that you are editing the original structure and anything connected is at risk if you manually change these things.

ko.utils.arrayGetDistinctValues ()

The `ko.utils.arrayGetDistinctValues` method allows you to take an array and remove duplicate values, leaving only distinct items. This time we will be dealing with a result set that is an array, so again in the View we will be using the foreach method on our `data-bind` attribute:

```
<h3>arrayMap() : All ages sorted</h3>
<ul data-bind="foreach: allYears">
  <li><span data-bind="text: $data"></span></li>
</ul>
<h3>arrayGetDistinctValues() : Unique ages</h3>
<ul data-bind="foreach: uniqueYears">
  <li><span data-bind="text: $data"></span></li>
</ul>
```

You may have noticed that we are inserting two segments this time. This is because `arrayGetDistintValues` modifies another array. We need the array it is going to modify. What we will do is create an array of all the ages using our `arrayMap` method, and then create another result with only the distinct values in it. In our script code, we again need to set `arrayGetDistinctValues` before the `applyBindings` command:

```
vm.allYears = ko.computed(function(){
  return allYears = ko.utils.arrayMap(vm.arr(),function(item){
    return item.age();
```

```
    });
  }); // arrayMap()
  vm.uniqueYears = ko.computed(function(){
    return ko.utils.arrayGetDistinctValues(vm.allYears().sort(),vm);
  }); // arrayGetDistinctValues()
```

Here is a screenshot of both sets of results:

arrayMap() : All ages sorted

- 23
- 32
- 46
- 46
- 54
- 63

arrayGetDistinctValues() : Unique ages

- 23
- 32
- 46
- 54
- 63

The first set was sorted in the call to the unique value set. This is something to watch out for as it can be confusing when something like this happens. We included it here for some food for thought and to illustrate, again, the need to be aware that you might be performing a command on the original set of data. If you were to follow best practice you might sort the results of the unique years, if that was your goal, rather than sorting the input data within the method. This is also an example of where an external variable is visible even though the sort call happened within the method arguments.

ko.utils.arrayForEach()

The `ko.utils.arrayForEach` method will allow you to loop through an array. This can be great for doing totals or other logic pulled from a summary of looking at individual objects. You could return all workers with children, for instance. While the most ideal place may be to do this coming from the database, this does not make it the only place it can ever be done. It is good practice to review where and why we do things to make sure our apps are performing and can scale as much as needed.

Our View code this time will be using a non-array value so we will not be using a foreach method. The reason we bring that up again here is if you use a wrong method your page will fail to run correctly. Often, the issue is as simple as trying to call an array method on a non-array property of the ViewModel. This is the kind of routine issue that can challenge any developer. Here is the View code:

```
<h3>arrayForEach() : total ages</h3>
Total Age: <span data-bind="text: totalAge"></span>
```

Just in case you missed me saying this somewhere in this book, let me make a point. In Knockout, a little bit of code has a lot of power. Here is the code for our total age processing:

```
vm.totalAge = ko.computed(function(){
  var years = 0;
  ko.utils.arrayForEach(vm.arr(), function(item){
    years += item.age();
  });
  return years;
}); // arrayForEach();
```

And of course, we get a total of the ages in our screenshot as follows:

arrayForEach() : total ages

Total Age: 264

ko.utils.compareArrays()

This allows you to compare arrays and return a collection, showing all items from both arrays. If the item did not exist in the second collection it will be shown as deleted. If the item is in the second set but not in the first set it will be shown as added. The return set will also show the index of the item where it exists.

Here is our View code for the last array example on `compareArrays`:

```
<h3>compareArrays() : 2 Color Arrays</h3>
<ul data-bind="foreach: diff">
  <li><span data-bind="text: $data.value + ' was ' +
  $data.status"></span></li>
</ul>
```

Our script code is once again simple, and hopefully by working through coding each of these by hand, they have become more natural to you also. Here is the `script` code:

```
vm.diff = ko.computed(function(){
    return ko.utils.compareArrays(vm.color_1(),vm.color_2());
}); // compareArrays()
```

Here is the screenshot of our code running:

compareArrays() : 2 Color Arrays

- red was retained
- green was deleted
- blue was retained
- orange was retained
- purple was added

We wanted to include a console log from the browser developer tools as we thought Chrome showed the structure nicely:

```
> ko.utils.compareArrays(vm.color_1(),vm.color_2())
< [▼ Object            , ▼ Object           , ▶ Object , ▶ Object , ▶ Object ]
      status: "retained"      index: 1
      value: "red"            status: "deleted"
    ▶ __proto__: Object       value: "green"
                            ▶ __proto__: Object
```

Purifying our computations

Now we are going to redo the `script` section of code using `pureComputed` versus `computed`. The term `pureComputed` was inspired by the concept of pure functions as a style of programming. It is nothing you need to understand to use so don't get caught up with the semantics of the name as there is no practical win as far as learning how these pure computations benefit us here.

When Knockout has something watching, a computed item is called a subscriber. Thus, it is considered to be a subscriber dependency. If we use the `pureComputed` method versus the `computed` method, Knockout will not calculate the value when there are no subscribers. This, of course, adds more speed to our processes by reducing calculations that aren't needed and unnecessary code from running. It is also another way to avoid any chance of memory issues.

When there are no subscribers, a pure computed observable is considered to be **sleeping**. When there are subscribers it is considered to be **listening**. The term listening is a bit odd for me as to me it would be **responding**. It does make sense though, because it is a computing method. So it does need to listen to the values it is using to compute with. If any of those values change it needs to recalculate its results.

Here is the updated script code moved to the better `pureComputed` method:

```
<script>
var vm = {};
jQuery.getJSON('utility.json').done(function(data){
  vm = ko.mapping.fromJS( data );
  vm.youngStaff = ko.pureComputed(function(){
    return ko.utils.arrayFilter(vm.arr(), function(item){
      if(item.age() < 35) { return true; }
      return false;
    });
  });
  vm.firstRetire = ko.pureComputed(function(){
    return ko.utils.arrayFirst(vm.arr(), function(item){
      if(item.age() > 45) return true;
      return false;
    });
  }); // arrayFirst
  vm.tillRetire = ko.pureComputed(function(){
    return ko.utils.arrayMap(vm.arr(),function(item){
      return 65 - item.age() + ' years till retirement.';
    })
  }); // arrayMap()
  vm.tillRetire2 = ko.pureComputed(function(){
    ko.utils.arrayMap(vm.arr(),function(item){
      item.yearsLeft = 65 -I tem.age() + ' years till
retirement.';
    })
  }); // arrayMap()
  vm.allYears = ko.pureComputed(function(){
    return allYears = ko.utils.arrayMap(vm.arr(),function(item){
      return item.age();
    });
  }); // arrayMap()
  vm.uniqueYears = ko.pureComputed(function(){
    return ko.utils.arrayGetDistinctValues(vm.allYears().sort(),vm);
  }); // arrayGetDistinctValues()
  vm.totalAge = ko.pureComputed(function(){
    var years = 0;
    ko.utils.arrayForEach(vm.arr(), function(item){
      years += item.age();
    });
```

```
    return years;
  }); // arrayForEach();
  vm.diff = ko.pureComputed(function(){
    return ko.utils.compareArrays(vm.color_1(),vm.color_2());
  }); // compareArrays()
  ko.applyBindings(vm);
});
</script>
```

If you want to know how many dependencies an item has, you can look at the `getDependenciesCount` method. Type the following into your console in your browser developer tools:

vm.allYears.getDependenciesCount()

This will show you how many items are subscribing to the `allYears` computed method. There is also a function that will tell us the number of items that are subscribing to the `allYears` calculation method, as follows:

vm.allYears.getSubscriptionsCount()

Coding documents for computed observables

We have included the following documents about observables just for reference here. While these were available online on the KnockoutJS site, it seemed like a good idea to include them here so you don't have to keep jumping between the website and the book.

A computed observable can be constructed using one of the following forms.

Form 1

The `ko.computed( evaluator [, targetObject, options] )` form supports the most common case of creating a computed observable. It has the following attributes:

- `evaluator`: This is a function that is used to evaluate the computed observable's current value.

- `targetObject`: If given, it defines the value of `this` whenever Knockout invokes your callback functions.

- `options`: This is an object with further properties for the computed observable. See the full list in the following section.

Form 2

The `ko.computed( options )` parameter, is a single parameter form for creating a computed observable that accepts a JavaScript object with any of the following properties:

- `read`: This is a required function and used to evaluate the computed observable's current value.

- `write`: This is an optional function and if given, this makes the computed observable writable. This function receives values that other code is trying to write to your computed observable. It's up to you to supply custom logic to handle the incoming values, typically by writing the values to some underlying observable(s).

- `owner`: This is an optional function and, if given, it defines the value of `this` whenever Knockout invokes your `read` or `write` callbacks.

- `pure`: This is optional and if this is true, the computed observable will be set up as `purecomputed observable`. This option is an alternative to the `ko.pureComputed` constructor.

- `deferEvaluation`: This is optional and if this option is true, then the value of the computed observable will not be evaluated until something actually attempts to access its value or manually subscribes to it. By default, a computed observable has its value determined immediately during creation.

- `disposeWhen`: This is an optional function and if given, this function is executed before each re-evaluation to determine if the computed observable should be disposed. A true-ish result will trigger disposal of the computed observable.

- `disposeWhenNodeIsRemoved`: This is an optional function. If given, disposal of the computed observable will be triggered when the specified DOM node is removed by Knockout. This feature is used to dispose computed observables used in bindings when nodes are removed by the template and control-flow bindings.

Form 3

The `ko.pureComputed( evaluator [, targetObject] )` form constructs `pure computed observable` using the given evaluator function and optional object to use for `this`. Unlike `ko.computed`, this method doesn't accept an `options` parameter.

Form 4

The `ko.pureComputed( options )` form constructs a pure computed observable using an `options` object. This accepts the `read`, `write`, and `owner` options described previously.

Using a computed observable

A computed observable provides the following functions:

- `dispose()`: This manually disposes the computed observable, clearing all subscriptions to dependencies. This function is useful if you want to stop a computed observable from being updated or want to clean up memory for a computed observable that has dependencies on observables that won't be cleaned.

- `extend(extenders)`: This applies the given extenders to the computed observable.

- `getDependenciesCount()`: This returns the current number of dependencies of the computed observable.

- `getSubscriptionsCount()`: This returns the current number of subscriptions (either from other computed observables or manual subscriptions) of the computed observable.

- `isActive()`: This returns whether the computed observable may be updated in the future. A computed observable is inactive if it has no dependencies.

- `peek()`: This returns the current value of the computed observable without creating a dependency.

- `subscribe( callback [,callbackTarget, event] )`: This registers `manual subscription` to be notified of changes to the computed observable.

Using the computed context

During the execution of a computed observable's evaluator function, you can access `ko.computedContext` to get information about the current computed property. It provides the following functions:

- `isInitial()`: This is a function that returns true if called during the first ever evaluation of the current computed observable, or false otherwise. For `pure` computed observables, `isInitial()` is always undefined.

- `getDependenciesCount()`: This returns the number of dependencies of the computed observable detected so far during the current evaluation.

 The `ko.computedContext.getDependenciesCount()` function is equivalent to calling `getDependenciesCount()` on the computed observable itself. The reason that it also exists on `ko.computedContext` is to provide a way of counting the dependencies during the first ever evaluation, before the computed observable has even finished being constructed.

Summary

This chapter opens up a whole load of features and options to make web style coding powerful and elegant. Learning to let a library handle things for you is hard for some but that perspective is ironic as we are programming computers for others to let our work manage things for them. This chapter has added several valuable skills and options to our knowledge and experience:

- We have learned to integrate data management in Knockout using JSON as an alternate way to pass data in and out.
- We have seen the incredible power of mapping to make our code another magnitude of elegant using Knockout.
- We have been introduced to the basics of using AJAX with Knockout.
- We have learned how to use utility functions for more advanced collection features, and again with less lines of code.
- Lastly, we learned how to improve the performance of our ViewModel using pure oriented compute functions (with a bonus clip of compute documents from the KnockoutJS online documents).

In our next chapter we will be looking at another way of packaging things to make our code shorter, more approachable, and more sustainable. Templates were once the domain of backend servers. The next chapter will show you why you need to do less on the backend and more on the frontend than ever before!

5
The Joy of Templates

A quick walk through history tells the story of how server-side code turned templates into magic. Data mixed with these templates and returned meaningful HTML for the client. These templates dynamically adapted to produce flexible and functional custom HTML pages. Along came AJAX and robbed the developer of this powerful approach to coding. But wait, templates are back again! Now they run at the client side. This chapter will teach you how to create the magic at the client side with Knockout. In this chapter, we will focus on:

- Native templates
- Enhanced collection handling
- Render events
- Third-party templates
- Awesome template options

Knockout is not just about two-way binding. Done right, it is about more elegant and sustainable code. We will learn how to come around for another layer of making our page creation simpler as we learn to use the power of templating in KnockoutJS.

Native templates

Templates are patterns for how we merge data and the stuff the data fits into. The most popular form of templates on computers in the early days was something we called a mail merge. Programs like Microsoft Word would use a mail merge document and a data file, and merge them together. The original purpose was for printing.

Over the time, we shifted to using this same type of technology to do web pages. When a user would go to a website and request a web page, the servers started getting smarter. The data was mixed into a template and the merged result was returned to the browser as HTML. This was an amazing game changer for shopping sites and other sites where the basic page was the same. This is why we call these pieces of code templates.

One way to look at this is to think about when people decorate houses. We have things we call stencils. While the stencil defines how the shape of the result will look, it does not control what color you paint something with. If you have an apple stencil you can paint a red apple, a green Granny Smith style apple, a yellow Golden Delicious apple, or go off standard and have a purple and yellow striped apple. The stencil only controls the container the content will be placed in.

In the same fashion, web templates frame the content. Well, mostly. You see, this is a program and it's a bit smarter than a wall painting stencil; so we can add in conditional logic and do things like repeat information or conditionally choose if we want to show any information at all. This is the power of a template.

We will have a bit more complex data set in this chapter because we want to get ourselves in touch with more real-life site pages, which we will be using outside this book. Here is the code section for this page. Not all the data will be used here. We will expand on the data as we progress through the chapter, so just focus on the stuff we actually use:

```
var mySeminar = {
  guest1 : { name: "Pete", seating: "standard" },
  guest2 : { name: "Re-Pete", seating: "balcony" },
  conference : {
    name: "KnockOut 2K",
    byLine: "MVVM That Works"
  }, speakers : [
    { id: 1, name: "John Doe", bio: 'This is the bio for John.',
      skills: [ "jQuery","KnockoutJS","SammyJS","NodeJS" ] },
    { id: 2, name: "Mary Smith", bio: 'This is the bio for Mary.',
      skills: [ "jQuery","KnockoutJS","PHP" ] },
    { id: 3, name: "TBA", bio: 'This is the bio for ???.',
      skills: [ "HTML5","SQL","JavaScript" ] }
  ], sessions : [
    { name: "SPA Applications", speakerId: 1 },
    { name: "MVVM Best Practices", speakerId: 1 },
    { name: "Mapping Madness", speakerId: 2 },
    { name: "Custom Components", speakerId: 2 },
    { name: "Browser Database for Beginners", speakerId: 3 }
  ]
```

```
};
vm = ko.mapping.fromJS(mySeminar);
ko.applyBindings( vm );
```

You probably guessed, looking at our data, that we will be showing a pseudo, meaning fake in this case but pseudo sounds so much nicer, seminar page. One thing you should realize is that data will come in all kinds of forms. You may need to arrange data before it works best for your pages. Don't think there is any strict pattern here that you have to follow. If you need to rearrange your data that is part of any template approach to code, you can do it.

Now, I said this section was going to be about native templates. This means you are going to create these templates in, the standard Knockout way of creating templates. This is what you should do most of the time. We will show later how to integrate external template libraries; but let me say right up front that in the real world this is a very rare approach to how developers use templates on Knockout pages.

Knockout follows the approach most browser-side templates are using. The actual template is nested inside a set of script tags. If you are new to this and are wondering why there is no JavaScript error when doing this, let me explain. In days past Microsoft Internet Explorer used a script called VBScript. Most other browsers used a script called JavaScript. Today we are seeing some other scripts come out on Internet Explorer again. TypeScript is an example, but it seems to require Visual Studio to function correctly and does not work as a native script; so staying with JavaScript for portability seems the way to go. These tags created a way to declare the type of content within them. If the content is not recognized, it is essentially ignored.

When the script is ignored, it means there is no DOM created from the markup code. JavaScript can still see this code though. So by declaring a different type attribute we are able to convert nested HTML into actionable code to use for our templates. This also allows us to actually use the familiar HTML scripting. Many people use something like jQuery to create content but it is nowhere near as elegant as a template approach. In fact, for a season, jQuery had its own templating. It pulled back with the reasoning that templates were not part of its solution focus.

Here is the first template we will use for our page. We will need to include the Knockout and mapping library for the code example here. The mapping library is not needed to do the template code. We are using it just to make our examples simpler. This makes for a focused approach on the subject and less coding for you as you go through the book.

```html
<script type="text/html" id="guest-template">
    <h3 data-bind="text: name"></h3>
    <p>Seating: <span data-bind="text: seating"></span></p>
</script>
```

You will notice that we put an `id` attribute on our template code segment. Each template will need a unique ID to work properly. Inside our template this looks pretty identical to the Knockout code we have been seeing all through this book. This is one of the great things about Knockout templating. It builds on what you already know and use with hardly any exceptions. An important consideration when doing templates is that the template should come before the actual call to binding the ViewModel. Following are the two external libraries we will include to make this page work. The `script` tag can come before or after them. It only needs to come before the binding call to prevent issues.

```
<script src="/share/js/knockout.js"></script>
<script src="/share/js/knockout.mapping.js"></script>
```

The last thing we need to do, to use template binding, is place a call to the template within the code. A template is similar to the wall stencil. You get to choose what you put inside the pattern. You get to choose what is merged into the template. This means you have to have data that matches the template. In this template, you need to pass in a ViewModel structure that contains structure items for name and seating. Here is a call to the template with the data declared:

```
<div data-bind="template: { name: 'guest-template', data: guest1
    }"></div>
```

If you have a template you want to use that doesn't have any data merges, you could reuse it on the page. I am not sure why you would want to do that but it is possible. Notice that with passing data to the template we are using the classic JSON format approach to what gets passed in. Let's modify the preceding code just a bit farther and have two templates with different data passed in, and a little markup near the templates:

```
<h2>Guests</h2>
These are the guests:
<div data-bind="template: { name: 'guest-template', data: guest1
    }"></div>
<div data-bind="template: { name: 'guest-template', data: guest2
    }"></div>
```

Notice that we have used our template twice in a row with the only difference being they have a different ViewModel structure passed through to them. You should also notice that the template name is the value of the `id` attribute in our scripted template declaration. Here is the resulting screenshot for this template:

Guests

These are the guests:

Pete

Seating: standard

Re-Pete

Seating: balcony

Since name and seating are variables of the structure, the scope is automatically understood by the template merging. It is a common practice to call the merging of the data with the template rendering, if you hear the term.

The actual data we merged to our template, before being inserted into the ViewModel, is as follows:

```
guest1 : { name: "Pete", seating: "standard" }
```

Well, we can now see our data being mixed with the template fast and easy. If we go to our browser developer tools to reach the console, we can input the following command. We want to modify the data inside our ViewModel to see if the binding has an instant effect on our View:

```
vm.guest1.name('Peter')
```

When we do this, notice the template smartly and immediately updates the content. So we see our data binding is locked into templates just like the binding outside of templates. There are different templates out in the open source market. What makes Knockout powerful is that it binds the rendered content to regenerate when the connected data changes. There have been a few comparisons of frameworks, and Knockout also performed better than others in terms of speed for this type of functionality. So, unless you are doing something incredibly large, having this run live should not greatly affect your user experience. With that said, don't forget to test performance as that is always the best practice. Here is the updated screenshot:

Guests

These are the guests:

Peter

Seating: standard

Re-Pete

Seating: balcony

Well, where are Pete, or Peter at the moment, and Re-Pete guests? That is our next block of code. We already have the data but the part of the data we will be using is this segment:

```
conference : {
    name: "KnockOut 2K",
    byLine: "MVVM That Works"
}
```

Here is the code for the display and the template that binds to it:

```
<h2>Seminar</h2>
<div data-bind="template: { name: 'tmpl-Seminar', data: conference }"></div>
```

We will need another template to demonstrate the merging of a different set of data. Here is the code for that template:

```
<script type="text/html" id="tmpl-Seminar">
    <h3 data-bind="text:name"></h3>
    <p>Theme: <span data-bind="text:byLine"></span></p>
</script>
```

Notice that our first template used a variable called name. In this template, we are also using a variable called name. Each template, when rendered, will look just at the data passed to it to merge the contents. Here is the screenshot from the template rendered to the page in this example:

There is no basic limit to the number of templates you can use on a page or the amount of data that can be merged. We are not going to assume that some developer or some client request could not go over the top. Yet, browsers and computers are so fast that these issues will rarely be something to focus on. The only time they may become an issue is if you are doing something complex with a variable that is in your ViewModel, and it is based on a computed value with complex logic. But I have not found a case so far where it is an issue in work, my company has produced for our clients.

Enhanced collection handling

In our first segment, native templates, we focused on single sets of data. In JavaScript, we often have collections of data stored in arrays. We will be including an example here to show how to use templates stored in arrays.

We can copy the data from our last example page to this page. We will be using more of the structure this time around. We will start by focusing on the speakers. This array contains structured items for each speaker. The code section of our `script` tag should look like this:

```
vm = ko.mapping.fromJS(mySeminar);
ko.applyBindings( vm );
```

If you think this looks basically the same as the last example of code, you are right. It will change soon, but we are looking to make a point here. Arrays and non-arrays are not coded differently for routine binding functionality. Here is the segment of data that we will be using for this part of the exercise:

```
speakers : [
  { id: 1, name: "John Doe", bio: 'This is the bio for John.',
    skills: [ "jQuery","KnockoutJS","SammyJS","NodeJS" ] },
  { id: 2, name: "Mary Smith", bio: 'This is the bio for Mary.',
    skills: [ "jQuery","KnockoutJS","PHP" ] },
  { id: 3, name: "TBA", bio: 'This is the bio for ???.',
    skills: [ "HTML5","SQL","JavaScript" ] }
],
```

We will be mixing this data with the following template structure and it will be enhanced as we go:

```
<script type="text/html" id="tmpl-Speakers">
  <h3 data-bind="text:name"></h3>
  <p>Bio: <span data-bind="text:bio"></span></p>
</script>
```

Here, we see the name and bio will be mixed into our page, pulling the name and bio from the data of each collection record. Here is the template call we will use on our page:

```
<h2>Speakers</h2>
<div data-bind="template: { name: 'tmpl-Speakers', foreach:
  speakers, as: 'speaker' }"></div>
```

This time we are using foreach rather than data in our template code. When using data it will pass in the entire data structure once. Using foreach will pass in the data structure as one collection item at a time. The template actually has no awareness of how the data is being passed to it. This is controlled by how we call the template. Here is the result we will see when run the code:

> # Speakers
>
> ## John Doe
> Bio: This is the bio for John.
>
> ## Mary Smith
> Bio: This is the bio for Mary.
>
> ## TBA
> Bio: This is the bio for ???.

Well, that was collection handling; but this section is called enhanced collection handling. We are going to go a little deeper and while using Knockout, we are still going to keep things pretty simple and the code very light.

As you can see in the following code, nested inside each speaker record, there is another simple collection of speaker skills. Here is the first item in the collection for clarity:

```
{ id: 1, name: "John Doe", bio: 'This is the bio for John.',
    skills: [ "jQuery","KnockoutJS","SammyJS","NodeJS" ] },
```

We see that John Doe has skills in using jQuery, KnockoutJS, SammyJS, and NodeJS. This is a JavaScript dude! He probably has other talents that he didn't list, but we can only show the ones he gave us, of course. How do we go about doing this? Well, one of the sweet powers of Knockout templates is the ability to nest other template calls inside templates. Here is the new template we will add to show the skills:

```
<script type="text/html" id="tmpl-SpeakerSkills">
    <li data-bind="text:skill"></li>
</script>
```

We will obviously need to modify the primary template to have this work. We are using an HTML list to show the skills, so we will need to nest the list in a list wrapper tag. We are also going to want to add a heading to clarify what this list represents. Here is our modified template with the new code highlighted:

```
<script type="text/html" id="tmpl-Speakers">
  <h3 data-bind="text:name"></h3>
  <p>Bio: <span data-bind="text:bio"></span></p>
  <h4>Skills</h4>
  <ul data-bind="template: { name: 'tmpl-SpeakerSkills', foreach:
  $data.skills, as: 'skill' }"></ul>
</script>
```

Notice that there is another foreach template binding, as the data being passed in is a collection. The last time it was a collection of structures and this time it is a collection of simple values. It does not matter to Knockout what type of items exist in the collection. It needs to be a collection or rather an array you designate when using the `foreach` passing of data.

The original call to the speaker template does need to be modified. Here is what our first speaker record looks like now. Of course, all the other records also have the added skills, but we wanted to conserve space; so please make sure you are doing all these examples in the browser, with code you entered by hand, to maximize your learning experience.

John Doe

Bio: This is the bio for John.

Skills

- jQuery
- KnockoutJS
- SammyJS
- NodeJS

This is pretty good but it is not good enough. We promised to cover enhanced collection template techniques and there is one more thing we want to show you. Nesting is the simplest form of enhancing our collection templates. Now, we want to show you how to do some relational data handling with the session records. Here is the session records data segment we will be mixing in:

```
sessions : [
  { name: "SPA Applications", speakerId: 1 },
  { name: "MVVM Best Practices", speakerId: 1 },
```

```
    { name: "Mapping Madness", speakerId: 2 },
    { name: "Custom Components", speakerId: 2 },
    { name: "Browser Database for Beginners", speakerId: 3 }
]
```

You should have noted that the speakerId attribute is part of this data collection. This is how we will tie the records in. It will take a minor amount of code to tie this in correctly, but it truly is a minor amount of code. We will need to add the following highlighted code to make this work. We have added this code between our mapping and binding:

```
vm = ko.mapping.fromJS(mySeminar);
vm.speakerSessions = function(speakerId){
  var mySessions = [];
  ko.utils.arrayMap(vm.sessions(),function(session){
    if(speakerId() == session.speakerId()){
      mySessions.push(session);
    }
  });
  return mySessions;
};
```

This time we are not using a collection to pass to the template; well, not a bound array collection. We will be calling the data by triggering a function that will filter and return an array collection. This means that as long as we are passing an array when the call is made, the template call does not care.

We are also using the arrayMap method of our Knockout utilities to filter data versus filter down. Notice that we call by designation the ViewModel as the first argument of the filter. It will then pass in each session item one at a time to see if the item should be placed in the filtered collection. Then, it will return the results. Pretty simple code. Oh, yes, it does receive the speakerId attribute as an argument when calling. That is key to making things work. Take a look at the following script code:

```
<script type="text/html" id="tmpl-SpeakerSessions">
  <h4>Sessions</h4>
  <ul data-bind="foreach:$root.speakerSessions(id)">
    <li data-bind="text:name() +' with '+ speaker.name()"></li>
  </ul>
</script>
```

Notice that we have used the $root designation to call our method. This is because we wanted to remind you that because this is a nested template, we need to make sure our method call is at the right level. The $root designation allows you to address the actual root level of the ViewModel. The ID that is passed in matches the speaker data item. The speakerSessions code we added will then match that ID with the records that have the same ID. If there is more than one session, it will show them.

We will need to also include a nested call to the sessions in our primary template for this to work. Again, we will not need to modify the original call to the speakers. Here is the code with the new part highlighted:

```
<script type="text/html" id="tmpl-Speakers">
  <h3 data-bind="text:name"></h3>
  <p>Bio: <span data-bind="text:bio"></span></p>
  <div data-bind="template: { name: 'tmpl-SpeakerSessions', data:
  $data }"></div>
  <h4>Skills</h4>
  <ul data-bind="template: { name: 'tmpl-SpeakerSkills', foreach:
  $data.skills, as: 'skill' }"></ul>
</script>
```

Take a moment and look at the code; discover the difference between the call to our additional nested template and the first nested template. You will see that in our additional method we did not pass in the data using the foreach designator. This time we used the data designator to pass in our collection. Both of these are valid approaches, but we wanted to give you examples of doing both for your experience.

Here is the resulting first record (again, not showing everything to save space). Notice how this time the nested template is handling the foreach designator using classic binding for Knockout:

John Doe

Bio: This is the bio for John.

Sessions

- SPA Applications with John Doe
- MVVM Best Practices with John Doe

Skills

- jQuery
- KnockoutJS
- SammyJS
- NodeJS

Render event handling

One of the things you grow to appreciate as your experience grows is the ability to do event handling. I have not needed this functionality yet with Knockout code in the live sites we have built; but it is awesome to know it is there if we do need it.

We will be using the following code this time. We will use a different data set for this example to keep our code simpler and focus on just this section:

```
<script>
    var ViewModel = function(){
        seasons = ko.observableArray([
            { name: 'Spring', months: [ 'March', 'April', 'May' ]
},
            { name: 'Summer', months: [ 'June', 'July', 'August' ]
},
            { name: 'Autumn', months: [ 'September', 'October',
'November' ] },
            { name: 'Winter', months: [ 'December', 'January',
'February' ] }
        ]);
    showRendered = function(e){
      $(e).wrapInner("<em style='color:green'></em>");
      };
      };
    vm = new ViewModel();
      ko.applyBindings(vm);
</script>
```

This also tells us that we will not always consider the mapping to be the best method. It is usually best in the early prototyping of pages to use mapping as it speeds up the creation of the stuff we need. Then, we migrate, if needed, to a non-mapped ViewModel when appropriate, to maximize productivity. If your experience varies then follow your instinct and use the approach that works best in your group.

The data and binding are obvious by now. The function we added will use jQuery to perform a wrap of each designated item, rendered by Knockout with italics and in green. One pragmatic use I have thought of for this is a log of a unit test to make sure the output is what is expected. Regardless of what you use it for, it will show you a couple of things.

First, we are not totally disconnected from jQuery while using Knockout. There is a way I like to describe this to people who are anxious that using Knockout will eliminate the use of jQuery. Yes, I remember how hard JavaScript was for most people before jQuery. They both have different strengths. Knockout shines at data binding and jQuery shines at AJAX communications between the client and the server, as well as at DOM manipulation. Together, they make a great team with each having areas and different challenges that they are best suited to meet.

Here are the templates we will use in this example. We will be using nested templates again. This is the root template:

```html
<script type="text/html" id="seasonTemplate">
    <li>
        <strong data-bind="text: "></strong>
        <strong data-bind="text: name"></strong>
        <ul data-bind="template: { name: 'monthTemplate', foreach:
  months, as: 'month' , afterRender: showRendered}"></ul>
    </li>
</script>
```

We have called the months as nested template calls. While we could have just rendered all this with regular tags, it would not have shown us how the event handlers work. Look closely at the nested data binding in the template call and you will see a setting for `afterRender`. You will see it calls the function we added to our code. Since it is in the root template, it will not need to use the `$root` designator to correctly call the function method to handle the render event. Here is the nested template that it will call to render the month items:

```html
<script type="text/html" id="monthTemplate">
    <li>
        <span data-bind="text: month"></span>
        is in
        <span data-bind="text: season.name"></span>
    </li>
</script>
```

There is something special I wanted you to see here also. Noticed that we use the variable `season.name` in this template. We were able to address the parent's data structure from the nested template. The guys who wrote the Knockout library had many awesome moments putting things like this together. So, where is the season declared? Look at the actual call to the root template:

```html
<ul data-bind="template: { name: 'seasonTemplate', foreach:
  seasons, as: 'season' }"></ul>
```

You will see an as designator with the season string declared as the alias of the structure. So, we could use $data in the first level of the template, but it would not work right to use $data in the second level of the template. By declaring the alias season, we can use that in the nested child, and it will properly target the right data set. Awesome!

Now, when we look at our results we get things properly handled and rendered. I admit that while I have used jQuery since just before Version 1.2, my history with Knockout was delayed more than that. If you are having issues with earlier versions that may not support every feature we are teaching here, jump into the online group. You will find it listed at the Knockout site. The community is awesome in how they support each other there.

Here is a screenshot of the results of this code:

- **Spring**
  - *March is in Spring*
  - *April is in Spring*
  - *May is in Spring*
- **Summer**
  - *June is in Summer*
  - *July is in Summer*
  - *August is in Summer*
- **Autumn**
  - *September is in Autumn*
  - *October is in Autumn*
  - *November is in Autumn*
- **Winter**
  - *December is in Winter*
  - *January is in Winter*
  - *February is in Winter*

Third-party template options

There was a time when jQuery was exploring creating its own templates, but that effort did not mature to a full release. So we will not cover that template here. The most popular template used with Knockout seems to have been **Underscore** as a result. Personally, before jumping into Knockout my template of choice was, well is, **Handlebars**. Yet, I have enjoyed Knockout templates so much that it has never compelled me to go as far as integrating Handlebars with Knockout yet.

I have played around with Underscore just to get a taste of why others use Underscore with Knockout; to see if I was missing something. It came down to a developer style difference that some developers like to use the Underscore style of template coding and others prefer to use native Knockout templates. In this section, we will be honoring the Underscore fans' approach.

We suggest some copy and paste from the done directory of the example code for this to prevent typos. If you are awesome enough, just go ahead and type this in though. Remember again, your examples should be going into the do folder for each chapter.

Here is our base code for this example:

```
<script>
var viewModel = {
    people: ko.observableArray([
        { name: ko.observable('Rod'), age: ko.observable(123) },
        { name: ko.observable('Jane'), age: ko.observable(125) },
        { name: ko.observable('Mary'), age: ko.observable(25) }
    ])
};
ko.applyBindings(viewModel);
</script>
```

Here is our code for calling the template:

```
<h1>People</h1>
<ul data-bind="template: { name: 'peopleList' }"></ul>
```

Now, here is our template. You should notice that the style of the template is different here. If you are accustomed to Underscore, this will work great. If you are not using Underscore you should not assume the code in this template will be an example of native Knockout templates.

```
<script type="text/html" id="peopleList">
    <% _.each(people(), function(person) { %>
        <li>
            <b data-bind="text: person.name"></b> is <%=
  person.age() %> years old
        </li>
    <% }) %>
</script>
```

This screenshot shows that we will produce the following results. Wait! There is one piece missing, but we did want to show you the results first.

People

- **Rod** is 123 years old
- **Jane** is 125 years old
- **Mary** is 25 years old

As far as the end user is concerned, there is no difference. Using third-party templates is for the benefit of the developers. Well, if you are doing a contract that requires the use of Underscore, that would be another benefit to this approach as it would let you do the job with Underscore and Knockout, if permitted otherwise. It might be good to verify that in advance just to make sure.

Modified template handling with Underscore

Let me express my gratitude again and say thanks to the Knockout community on Google groups. This, in addition to several sites online, is where I learned how to do template handling. The technique allows us to manage the template engine and pass the results out to process through the Underscore engine. The key code is highlighted as follows:

```
/* ---- Begin integration of Underscore template engine with Knockout.
Could go in a separate file of course. ---- */
    ko.underscoreTemplateEngine = function () { }
    ko.underscoreTemplateEngine.prototype = ko.utils.extend(new
  ko.templateEngine(), {
        renderTemplateSource: function (templateSource,
  bindingContext, options) {
            // Precompile and cache the templates for efficiency
            var precompiled =
  templateSource['data']('precompiled');
            if (!precompiled) {
                precompiled = _.template("<% with($data) { %> " +
  templateSource.text() + " <% } %>");
                templateSource['data']('precompiled',
  precompiled);
            }
            // Run the template and parse its output into an array
  of DOM elements
```

```
        var renderedMarkup =
precompiled(bindingContext).replace(/\s+/g, " ");
            return ko.utils.parseHtmlFragment(renderedMarkup);
        },
        createJavaScriptEvaluatorBlock: function(script) {
            return "<%= " + script + " %>";
        }
    });
    ko.setTemplateEngine(new ko.underscoreTemplateEngine());
/* ---- End integration of Underscore template engine with
    Knockout ---- */
```

The first highlighted section passes the code and data into the Underscore template handler to be rendered by Underscore. Underscore does produce some results that need to be cleaned up to work right here, so the second highlighted section is there to clean up the rendered code.

Live updates and the subscribe method in Knockout

We are going to create the ability to add items with an edit form on the screen. Here is the markup for the View that we will add for this functionality:

```
<input data-bind="value: name" />
<input data-bind="value: age" />
<button data-bind="click: addItem">Add</button>
```

We will need to also add the ViewModel structure and it will include these items:

```
name: ko.observable(),
age: ko.observable(),

addItem: function() {
var item = { name: ko.observable(viewModel.name()), age:
  ko.observable(viewModel.age()) };
    viewModel.people.push(item);
    viewModel.name("");
    viewModel.age("");
}
```

When adding items or removing them, Knockout gives us the ability to monitor these changes, and that is what we wanted to illustrate. This is the code we use to tell Knockout we want to subscribe, or listen, to events. The particular event we will be listening to will be the arrayChange event on the people array collection. Here is the code for it. Notice that we are also dumping the results into the console. We also will be pushing the results of the changes to another attribute for the people changes.

```
viewModel.people.subscribe(function(e){
  console.log(e);
}, viewModel, "arrayChange");
viewModel.people.subscribe(viewModel.peopleChange, viewModel,
  "arrayChange");
```

The results that we pass into peopleChange, we will handle by converting them to JSON using the binding on the View as follows. Anytime our value in peopleChange is updated, the results will be displayed as a JSON structure.

```
<pre data-bind="text: ko.toJSON(peopleChange, null, 2)"></pre>
```

Now, just in case that was confusing on the first pass or you don't want to download the code, let me give you the markup View code here:

```
<h1>People</h1>
<ul data-bind="template: { name: 'peopleList' }"></ul>
<script type="text/html" id="peopleList">
    <% _.each(people(), function(person) { %>
        <li>
            <b data-bind="text: person.name"></b> is <%=
  person.age() %> years old
        </li>
    <% }) %>
</script>
<pre data-bind="text: ko.toJSON(peopleChange, null, 2)"></pre>
<input data-bind="value: name" />
<input data-bind="value: age" />
<button data-bind="click: addItem">Add</button>
```

It looks much simpler when all in one place; well, it does to me. There are more scripts included this time; here is the collection we need for this example:

```
<script
  src="https://ajax.googleapis.com/ajax/libs/jquery/1.11.0/jquery.mi
  n.js"></script>
<script
  src="//netdna.bootstrapcdn.com/bootstrap/3.1.1/js/bootstrap.min.js
  "></script>
```

```
<script src="/share/js/knockout.js"></script>
<script
  src="http://documentcloud.github.com/underscore/underscore-
  min.js"></script>
```

Yes, these do work with the current version of jQuery also, if you have that question. We will now show the code for this example page:

```
<script>
/* ---- Begin integration of Underscore template engine with
   Knockout. Could go in a separate file of course. ---- */
    ko.underscoreTemplateEngine = function () { }
    ko.underscoreTemplateEngine.prototype = ko.utils.extend(new
ko.templateEngine(), {
        renderTemplateSource: function (templateSource,
bindingContext, options) {
            // Precompile and cache the templates for efficiency
            var precompiled =
templateSource['data']('precompiled');
            if (!precompiled) {
                precompiled = _.template("<% with($data) { %> " +
templateSource.text() + " <% } %>");
                templateSource['data']('precompiled',
precompiled);
            }
            // Run the template and parse its output into an array
of DOM elements
            var renderedMarkup =
precompiled(bindingContext).replace(/\s+/g, " ");
            return ko.utils.parseHtmlFragment(renderedMarkup);
        },
        createJavaScriptEvaluatorBlock: function(script) {
            return "<%= " + script + " %>";
        }
    });
    ko.setTemplateEngine(new ko.underscoreTemplateEngine());
/* ---- End integration of Underscore template engine with
   Knockout ---- */
var viewModel = {
    people: ko.observableArray([
        { name: ko.observable('Rod'), age: ko.observable(123) },
        { name: ko.observable('Jane'), age: ko.observable(125) },
        { name: ko.observable('Mary'), age: ko.observable(25) }
    ]),
    peopleChange: ko.observable(),
```

```
        name: ko.observable(),
        age: ko.observable(),
        addItem: function() {
            var item = { name: ko.observable(viewModel.name()), age:
    ko.observable(viewModel.age()) };
            viewModel.people.push(item);
            viewModel.name("");
            viewModel.age("");
        },
        removeItem: function(item) {
            viewModel.people.remove(item);
        }
    };
    viewModel.people.subscribe(viewModel.peopleChange, viewModel,
      "arrayChange");
    viewModel.people.subscribe(function(e){
      console.log(e);
    }, viewModel, "arrayChange");
    ko.applyBindings(viewModel);
    </script>
```

Now, we have code that will show us third-party templates, subscriptions, and dynamic modification of the data stored in our binding. Here is what the screen will look like. Well, in my done version of the code it is wrapped in Bootstrap, so this is what it looks like in Bootstrap:

We will go ahead and add John to the list and make him 40 years old. Here is what you will see in the screenshot with the results of subscribe put out as a JSON structure. If a record had been deleted it would show that as well; another reason why Knockout is so flexible to work with. You will have also noticed in our code that as soon as we added the items to the structure of our data via the binding, we also cleared the input boxes to keep a clean interface for the user. Here is the resultant screenshot:

Let me say again that most people do not use third-party templates as the native templates are very powerful. This doesn't mean to do so is wrong, but the need to do so could be just a need to learn how to use the abilities of the native template. If that is the case, we hope this chapter has been the answer to that need.

Awesome template options

There is one more time someone may want to do something with templates different from the pure native style of using templates with Knockout. This is because you may like to use a slightly different kind of coding style. In this last section of the chapter, we will give you a few more options.

We are back to native templates; I thought we should mention that in case someone had a question. Here are the templates that we will be using on this page:

```html
<script type="text/html" id="guest-template">
    <h3>{{name}}</h3>
    <p>Seating: {{seating}}</p>
</script>
<script type="text/html" id="guest-template-alt">
    <h3>Others</h3>
    <p>Seating: General Seating</p>
</script>
```

```
<script type="text/html" id="tmpl-Seminar">
  <h3>{{name}}</h3>
  <p>Theme: {{byLine}}</p>
</script>
```

We will be using the data that we used from the beginning of the chapter with this example. Other than that, we will also be adding one more plugin library to this example. It is clearly one of my favorite Knockout libraries, the **Punches** library. After all, what would Knockout be without punches? So we need to include jQuery, Knockout, Knockout-mapping, and Knockout punches, and that will work for now.

Here is the binding data for our traditional template included on this page:

```
<h2>Guests</h2>
These are the guests:
<div data-bind="template: { name: 'guest-template', data: guest1
  }"></div>
<div data-bind="template: { name: 'guest-template', data: guest2
  }"></div>
```

Here is the output we get from this section of code on our page. If you took time to look at our templates, you may have noticed something different. The style of coding we used to tell our templates what variables we wanted to merge is now surrounded with double curly brackets. Yet, our output is just as we would expect without the need to dig in and use the data-bind attribute to deliver the results:

Now, we will take a look at Punches template syntax. We are including the code for the standard bindings to make sure someone does not assume that this is the code that belongs in the `script` tags. This is HTML code and should be added right to the View code on our page as follows:

```
<h2>Guests</h2>
These are the guests:
<div data-bind="template: { name: 'guest-template', data: guest1
  }"></div>
```

```
<div data-bind="template: { name: 'guest-template', data: guest2
    }"></div>
{{#template {name:'guest-template', data: guest1} /}}
{{#template {name:'guest-template', data: guest2} /}}
```

When you run the code again you will see **Pete** and **Re-Pete** are putting out the same results twice. Some people, because of their personal style, may prefer the Punches style of coding. You may have remembered that I mentioned my former favorite style of coding was Handlebars. This is similar to Handlebars coding syntax, so it works best for me; if it's not your style then just count it as a difference in developer personality. Here is the updated screenshot:

There is one other approach that I am using now to put templates on a page. I am using Knockout-powered custom tags. Well, sort of. They are modified with a library that, I call "KOmponents". You will learn more about Knockout custom tags in the next chapter, but it seemed fitting to show you one in action here. We will put the output on the page a third time. Here is the modified View markup:

```
<h2>Guests</h2>
These are the guests:
<div data-bind="template: { name: 'guest-template', data: guest1
    }"></div>
<div data-bind="template: { name: 'guest-template', data: guest2
    }"></div>
{{#template {name:'guest-template', data: guest1} /}}
{{#template {name:'guest-template', data: guest2} /}}
<kom-template data="guest1" template="'guest-template'"></kom-
    template>
<kom-template data="guest2" template="'guest-template'"></kom-
    template>
```

Here we go; run the code and you will see we get a third set of **Pete** and **Re-Pete** on the page. We will skip *repeating* another copy of **Pete** and **Re-Pete** in our screen images. The goal was to show you that they all put out the same content.

We will complete this by adding this to the bottom of our View markup below all the `guest-template` sections:

```
<hr>
{{#template 'guest-template-alt'/}}
<hr>
<h2>Seminar</h2>
<div data-bind="template: { name: 'tmpl-Seminar', data: conference
  }"></div>
```

These will put out the content of the templates with the following results. You see, we have chosen to use the Punches with the Handlebars-style approach in one of them again.

Others

Seating: General Seating

Seminar

KnockOut 2K

Theme: MVVM That Works

Summary

This chapter has given you a well-rounded introduction to Knockout templates. If you have never used templates before, we hope you appreciate the concept of templates. If you have used them before, we hope you like the richer data-bound auto-updating ability of templates using Knockout.

In this chapter we have learned what templates do and how to use them with Knockout. We have learned how to nest templates with collections and non-collection structures. We have learned how to use event triggers and mixed a little jQuery in to modify template results. We have also learned how to mix in third-party template technology, the concept of subscribing to observables, and a couple of extra ways to merge templates onto our page. We also learned to use an alternative style of binding with the Punches library.

In our next chapter, we will dive into the wonder of building our own custom HTML tags. Has there ever been a time when you thought that standard HTML tags were limited? You actually wanted to have some programmable interactive features of HTML-style tags? Jump into the next chapter and you will find what you are looking for in both cases.

6
Packaged Elegance

First there was HTML and JavaScript, then CSS. Next came AJAX to usher in
Web 2.0, as it is called. After that, templates drove us to a more dynamic, creative
platform. The next advancement in web development was custom HTML
components. KnockoutJS allows us to jump right in with some game-changing
elegance for designers and developers. In this chapter, we will focus on:

- An introduction to components
- **Bring Your Own Tags (BYOT)**
- Enhancing attribute handling
- Making your own libraries
- **Asynchronous module definition (AMD)** — on demand resource loading
- Component-based **Single-Page Applications (SPA)**

This entire chapter is about packaging your code for reuse. Using these techniques,
you can make your code more approachable and elegant.

Introduction to components

We hope you enjoyed learning about templates in the last chapter. Perhaps the best
explanation of a component is a packaged template with an isolated ViewModel.
Here is the syntax we would use to declare a `like` component on the page:

```
<div data-bind="component: "like"''"></div>
```

If you are passing no parameters through to the component, this is the correct
syntax. If you wish to pass parameters through, you would use a JSON style
structure as follows:

```
<div data-bind="component:
{name: 'like-widget',params:{ approve: like} }"></div>
```

This would allow us to pass named parameters through to our custom component. In this case, we are passing a parameter named `approve`. This would mean we had a bound `viewModel` variable by the name of `like`. Look at how this would be coded. Create a page called `components.html` using the `_base.html` file to speed things up as we have done in all our other chapters. In your `script` section, create the following ViewModel:

```
<script>
ViewModel = function(){
  self = this;
  self.like = ko.observable(true);
}
;
// insert custom component here
vm = new ViewModel();
ko.applyBindings(vm);
</script>
```

Now, we will create our custom component. Here is the basic component we will use for this first component. Place the code where the comment is, as we want to make sure it is added before our `applyBindings` method is executed:

```
ko.components.register('like-widget', {
  viewModel: function(params) {
    this.approve = params.approve;
    // Behaviors:
    this.toggle = function(){
      this.approve(!this.approve());
    }.bind(this);
  },
  template:
    '<div class="approve">\
      <button data-bind="click: toggle">\
        <span data-bind="visible: approve" class="glyphicon
glyphicon-thumbs-up"></span>\
        <span data-bind="visible:! approve()" class="glyphicon
glyphicon-thumbs-down"></span>\
      </button>\
    </div>'
});
```

There are two sections to our components: the `viewModel` and `template` sections. In the previous chapter, we learned how to use Knockout templates. In this chapter, we will be using those details inside the component.

The standard Knockout component passes variables to the component using the `params` structure. We can either use this structure or you could optionally use the *self* = *this* approach if desired. In addition to setting the variable structure, it is also possible to create behaviors for our components. If we look in the template code, we can see we have data-bound the click event to toggle the approve setting in our component. Then, inside the button, by binding to the visible trait of the `span` element, either the thumbs up or thumbs down image will be shown to the user. Yes, we are using a Bootstrap icon element rather than a graphic here. Here is a screenshot of the initial state:

When we click on the thumb image, it will toggle between the thumbs up and the thumbs down version. Since we also passed in the external variable that is bound to the page ViewModel, we see that the value in the matched span text will also toggle. Here is the markup we would add to the page to produce these results in the View section of our code:

```
<div data-bind="component:
    {name: 'like-widget', params:{ approve: like} }"></div>
<span data-bind="text: like"></span>
```

You could build this type of functionality with a jQuery plugin as well, but it is likely to take a bit more code to do two-way binding and match the tight functionality we have achieved here. This doesn't mean jQuery plugins are bad, as this is also a jQuery-related technology. What it does mean is we have ways to do things even better. It is this author's opinion that features like this would still make great additions to the core jQuery library. Yet, I am not holding my breath waiting for them to adopt a Knockout-type project to the wonderful collection of projects they have at this point, and do not feel we should hold that against them. Keeping focused on what they do best is one of the reasons libraries like Knockout can provide a wider array of options. It seems the decisions are working on our behalf even if they are taking a different approach than I expected.

Dynamic component selection

You should have noticed when we selected the component that we did so using a quoted declaration. While at first it may seem to be more constricting, remember that it is actually a power feature. By using a variable instead of a hardcoded value, you can dynamically select the component you would like to be inserted. Here is the markup code:

```
<div data-bind="component:
    { name: widgetName, params: widgetParams }"></div>
<span data-bind="text:widgetParams.approve"></span>
```

Notice that we are passing in both `widgetName` as well as `widgetParams`. Because we are binding the structure differently, we also need to show the bound value differently in our span. Here is the `script` part of our code that needs to be added to our `viewModel` code:

```
self.widgetName = ko.observable("like-widget");
self.widgetParams = {
  approve: ko.observable(true)
};
```

We will get the same visible results but notice that each of the like buttons is acting independent of the other. What would happen if we put more than one of the same elements on the page? If we do that, Knockout components will act independent of other components. Well, most of the time they act independent. If we bound them to the same variable they would not be independent. In your `viewModel` declaration code, add another variable called `like2` as follows:

```
self.like2 = ko.observable(false);
```

Now, we will add another like button to the page by copying our first like View code. This time, change the value from `like` to `like2` as follows:

```
<like-widget params="approve: like2"></like-widget>
<span data-bind="text: like2"></span>
```

This time when the page loads, the other likes display with a thumbs up, but this like will display with a thumbs down. The text will also show **false** stored in the bound value. Any of the like buttons will act independently because each of them is bound to unique values. Here is a screenshot of the third button:

Bring Your Own Tags (BYOT)

What is an element? Basically, an element is a component that you reach using the tag syntax. This is the way it is expressed in the official documentation at this point and it is likely to stay that way. It is still a component under the hood. Depending on the crowd you are in, this distinction will be more or less important. Mostly, just be aware of the distinction in case someone feels it is important, as that will let you be on the same page in discussions. Custom tags are a part of the forthcoming HTML feature called Web Components. Knockout allows you to start using them today. Here is the View code:

```
<like-widget params="approve: like3"></like-widget>
<span data-bind="text: like3"></span>
```

You may want to code some tags with a single tag rather than a double tag, as in an opening and closing tag syntax. Well, at this time, there are challenges getting each browser to see the custom element tags when declared as a single tag. This means custom tags, or elements, will need to be declared as opening and closing tags for now.

We will also need to create our `like3` bound variable for `viewModel` with the following code:

```
self.like3 = ko.observable(true);
```

Running the code gives us the same wonderful functionality as our `data-bind` approach, but now we are creating our own HTML tags. Has there ever been a time you wanted a special HTML tag that just didn't exist? There is a chance you could create that now using Knockout component element-style coding.

Enhancing attribute handling

Now, while custom tags are awesome, there is just something different about passing everything in with a single param attribute. The reason for this is that this process matches how our tags work when we are using the `data-bind` approach to coding. In the following example, we will look at passing things in via individual attributes. This is not meant to work as a `data-bind` approach, but it is focused completely on the custom tag element component.

The first thing you want to do is make sure this enhancement doesn't cause any issues with the normal elements. We did this by checking the custom elements for a standard prefix. You do not need to work through this code as it is a bit more advanced. The easiest thing to do is to include our Knockout components tag with the following `script` tag:

```
<script src="/share/js/knockout.komponents.js"></script>
```

In this tag, we have this code segment to convert the tags that start with `kom-` to tags that use individual attributes rather than a JSON translation of the attributes. Feel free to borrow the code to create libraries of your own. We are going to be creating a standard set of libraries on GitHub for these component tags. Since the HTML tags are Knockout components, we are calling these libraries "KOmponents". The resource can be found at `https://github.com/sosensible/komponents`.

Now, with that library included, we will use our View code to connect to the new tag. Here is the code to use in the View:

```
<kom-like approve="tagLike"></kom-like>
<span data-bind="text: tagLike"></span>
```

Notice that in our HTML markup, the tag starts with the library prefix. This will also require `viewModel` to have a binding to pass into this tag as follows:

```
self.tagLike = ko.observable(true);
```

The following is the code for the actual "attribute-aware version" of Knockout components. Do not place this in the code as it is already included in the library in the shared directory:

```
// <kom-like /> tag
ko.components.register('kom-like', {
  viewModel: function(params) {
    // Data: value must but true to approve
    this.approve = params.approve;
    // Behaviors:
    this.toggle = function(){
      this.approve(!this.approve());
    }.bind(this);
  },
  template:
    '<div class="approve">\
      <button data-bind="click: toggle">\
        <span data-bind="visible: approve" class="glyphicon
glyphicon-thumbs-up"></span>\
        <span data-bind="visible:! approve()" class="glyphicon
glyphicon-thumbs-down"></span>\
      </button>\
    </div>'
});
```

The tag in the View changed as we passed the information in via named attributes and not as a JSON structure inside a param attribute. We also made sure to manage these tags by using a prefix. The reason for this is that we did not want our fancy tags to break the standard method of passing params commonly practiced with regular Knockout components.

As we see, again we have another functional component with the added advantage of being able to pass the values in a style more familiar to those used to coding with HTML tags.

Building your own libraries

Again, we are calling our custom components KOmponents. We will be creating a number of library solutions over time and welcome others to join in. Tags will not do everything for us, as there are some limitations yet to be conquered. That doesn't mean we wait for all the features before doing the ones we can for now. In the previous chapter, we showed a KOmponent tag for using templates. That is also included in the base KOmponent library.

In this segment of the chapter, we will also be showing some tags from our Bootstrap KOmponents library. First we will need to include the Bootstrap KOmponents library:

```
<script src="/share/js/knockout.komponents.bs.js"></script>
```

Above viewModel in our script, we need to add a function to make this section of code simpler. At times, when passing items into observables, we can pass in richer bound data using a function like this. Again, create this function above the viewModel declaration of the script, shown as follows:

```
var listItem = function(display, students){
  this.display = ko.observable(display);
  this.students = ko.observable(students);
  this.type = ko.computed(function(){
    switch(Math.ceil(this.students()/5)){
      case 1:
      case 2:
        return 'danger';
        break;
      case 3:
        return 'warning';
        break;
      case 4:
        return 'info';
        break;
```

```
        default:
            return 'success';
    }
    },this);
};
```

Now, inside `viewModel`, we will declare a set of data to pass to a Bootstrap style `listGroup` as follows:

```
self.listData = ko.observableArray([
    new listItem("HTML5",12),
    new listItem("CSS",8),
    new listItem("JavaScript",19),
    new listItem("jQuery",48),
    new listItem("Knockout",33)
]);
```

Each item in our array will have display, students, and type variables. We are using a number of features in Bootstrap here but packaging them all up inside our Bootstrap smart tag. This tag starts to go beyond the bare basics. It is still very implementable, but we don't want to throw too much at you to absorb at one time, so we will not go into the detailed code for this tag. What we do want to show is how much power can be wrapped into custom Knockout tags. Here is the markup we will use to call this tag and bind the correct part of `viewModel` for display:

```
<kom-listgroup data="listData" badgeField="'students'"
    typeField="'type'"></kom-listgroup>
```

That is it. You should take note of a couple of special details. The data is passed in as a bound Knockout ViewModel. The badge field is passed in as a string name to declare the field on the data collection where the badge count will be pulled. The same string approach has been used for the type field. The type will set the colors as per standard Bootstrap types. The theme here is that if there are not enough students to hold a class, then it shows the danger color in the list group custom tag. Here is what it looks like in the browser when we run the code:

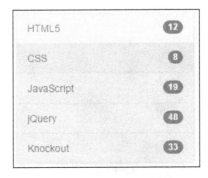

While this is neat, let's jump into our browser tools console and change the value of one of the items. Let's say there was a class on some cool web technology called jQuery. What if people had not heard of it and didn't know what it was and you really wanted to take the class? Well, it would be nice to encourage a few others to check it out. How would you know whether the class was at a danger level or not? Well, we could simply use the badge and the numbers, but how awesome is it to also use the color coding hint? Type the following code into the console and see what changes:

```
vm.listData()[3].display()
```

Because JavaScript starts counting with zero for the first item, we will get the following result:

```
> vm.listData()[3].display()
  "jQuery"
```

Now we know we have the right item, so let's set the student count to nine using the following code in the browser console:

```
vm.listData()[3].students(9)
```

Notice the change in the jQuery class. Both the badge and the type value have updated. This screenshot of the update shows how much power we can wield with very little manual coding:

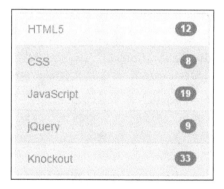

We should also take a moment to see how the type was managed. Using the functional assignment, we were able to use the Knockout computed binding for that value. Here is the code for that part again:

```
this.type = ko.computed(function(){
    switch(Math.ceil(this.students()/5)){
      case 1:
      case 2:
        return 'danger';
```

```
      break;
   case 3:
      return 'warning';
      break;
   case 4:
      return 'info';
      break;
   default:
      return 'success';
   }
},this);
```

While the code is outside the `viewModel` declaration, it is still able to bind properly to make our code run even inside a custom tag created with Knockout's component binding.

Bootstrap component example

Here is another example of binding with Bootstrap. The general best practice for using modal display boxes is to place them higher in the code, perhaps under the `body` tag, to make sure there are no conflicts with the rest of the code. Place this tag right below the `body` tag as shown in the following code:

```
<kom-modal id="'komModal'" title="komModal.title()"
   body="komModal.body()"></kom-modal>
```

Again, we will need to make some declarations inside `viewModel` for this to work right. Enter this code into the declarations of `viewModel`:

```
self.komModal = {
   title: ko.observable('Modal KOMponent'),
   body: ko.observable('This is the body of the <strong>modal
   KOMponent</strong>.')
};
```

We will also create a button on the page to call our `viewModel`. The button will use the binding that is part of Bootstrap. The `data-toggle` and `data-target` attributes are not Knockout binding features. Knockout works side-by-side wonderfully though. Another point of interest is the standard ID attribute, which tells how Bootstrap items, like this button, interact with the modal box. This is another reason it may be beneficial to use KOmponents or a library like it. Here is the markup code:

```
<button type="button" data-toggle="modal" data-
   target="#komModal">Open Modal KOmponent</button>
```

When we click on the button, this is the requestor we see:

Now, to understand the power of Knockout working with our requestor, head back over to your browser tools console. Enter the following command into the prompt:

```
vm.komModal.body("Wow, live data binding!")
```

The following screenshot shows the change:

Who knows what type of creative modular boxes we can build using this type of technology. This brings us closer towards creating what we can imagine. Perhaps it may bring us closer to building some of the wild things our customers imagine. While that may not be your main motivation for using Knockout, it would be nice to have a few less roadblocks when we want to be creative. It would also be nice to have this wonderful ability to package and reuse these solutions across a site without using copy and paste and searching back through the code when the client makes a change to make updates.

Again, feel free to look at the file to see how we made these components work. They are not extremely complicated once you get the basics of using Knockout and its components. If you are looking to build components of your own, they will help you get some insight on how to do things inside as you move your skills to the next level.

Understanding the AMD approach

We are going to look into the concept of what makes an AMD-style website. The point of this approach to sites is to pull content on demand. The content, or modules as they are defined here, does not need to be loaded in a particular order. If there are pieces that depend on other pieces, that is, of course, managed. We will be using the *RequireJS* library to manage this part of our code.

We will create four files in this example, as follows:

- `amd.html`
- `amd.config.js`
- `pick.js`
- `pick.html`

In our AMD page, we are going to create a configuration file for our RequireJS functionality. That will be the `amd.config.js` file mentioned in the aforementioned list. We will start by creating this file with the following code:

```
// require.js settings
var require = {
    baseUrl: ".",
    paths: {
        "bootstrap":        "/share/js/bootstrap.min",
        "jquery":           "/share/js/jquery.min",
        "knockout":         "/share/js/knockout",
        "text":             "/share/js/text"
    },
    shim: {
        "bootstrap": { deps: ["jquery"] },
        "knockout": { deps: ["jquery"] },
    }
};
```

We see here that we are creating some alias names and setting the paths these names point to for this page. The file could, of course, be working for more than one page, but in this case, it has specifically been created for a single page. The configuration in RequireJS does not need the `.js` extension on the file names, as you would have noted.

Now, we will look at our `amd.html` page where we pull things together. We are again using the standard page we have used for this course, which you will notice if you preview the `done` file example of the code. There are a couple of differences though, because the JavaScript files do not all need to be called at the start. RequireJS handles this well for us. We are not saying this is a standard practice of AMD, but it is an introduction of the concepts.

We will need to include the following three script files in this example:

```
<script src="/share/js/knockout.js"></script>
<script src="amd.config.js"></script>
<script src="/share/js/require.js"></script>
```

Notice that the configuration settings need to be set before calling the `require.js` library. With that set, we can create the code to wire Knockout binding on the page. This goes in our `amd.html` script at the bottom of the page:

```
<script>
ko.components.register('pick', {
  viewModel: { require: 'pick' },
  template: { require: 'text!pick.html' }
});
viewModel = function(){
  this.choice = ko.observable();
}
vm = new viewModel();
ko.applyBindings(vm);
</script>
```

Most of this code should look very familiar. The difference is that the external files are being used to set the content for `viewModel` and `template` in the `pick` component. The `require` setting smartly knows to include the `pick.js` file for the `pick` setting. It does need to be passed as a string, of course. When we include the template, you will see that we use `text!` in front of the file we are including. We also declare the extension on the file name in this case. The text method actually needs to know where the text is coming from, and you will see in our `amd.config.js` file that we created an alias for the inclusion of the text function.

Now, we will create the `pick.js` file and place it in the same directory as the `amd.html` file. It could have been in another directory, and you would have to just set that in the component declaration along with the filename. Here is the code for this part of our AMD component:

```
define(['knockout'], function(ko) {
    function LikeWidgetViewModel(params) {
        this.chosenValue = params.value;
        this.land = Math.round(Math.random()) ? 'heads' : 'tails';
    }
    LikeWidgetViewModel.prototype.heads = function() {
        this.chosenValue('heads');
    };
    LikeWidgetViewModel.prototype.tails = function() {
```

```
            this.chosenValue('tails');
    };
    return LikeWidgetViewModel;
});
```

Notice that our code starts with the `define` method. This is our AMD functionality in place. It is saying that before we try to execute this section of code we need to make sure the Knockout library is loaded. This allows us to do on-demand loading of code as needed. The code inside the `viewModel` section is the same as the other examples we have looked at with one exception. We return `viewModel` as you see at the end of the preceding code. We used the shorthand code to set the value for `heads` and `tails` in this example.

Now, we will look at our template file, `pick.html`. This is the code we will have in this file:

```
<div class="like-or-dislike" data-bind="visible: !chosenValue()">
<button data-bind="click: heads">Heads</button>
<button data-bind="click: tails">Tails</button>
</div>
<div class="result" data-bind="visible: chosenValue">
    You picked <strong data-bind="text: chosenValue"></strong>
    The correct value was <strong data-bind="text:
land"></strong>
</div>
```

This template follows the same concepts as the ones we looked at in the previous chapter. There is nothing special other than the code needed to make this example work. The goal is to allow a custom tag to offer up heads or tails options on the page. We also pass in a bound variable from `viewModel`. We will be passing it into three identical tags.

The tags are actually going to load the content instantly in this example. The goal is to get familiar with how the code works. We will take it to full practice at the end of the chapter. Right now, we will put this code in the View segment of our `amd.html` page:

```
<h2>One Choice</h2>
<pick params="value: choice"></pick><br>
<pick params="value: choice"></pick><br>
<pick params="value: choice"></pick>
```

Notice that we have included the `pick` tag three times. While we are passing in the bound choice item from `viewModel`, each tag will randomly choose heads or tails. When we run the code, this is what we will see:

Since we passed the same bound item into each of the three tags, when we click on any heads or tails set, it will immediately pass that value out to `viewModel`, which will in turn immediately pass the value back into the other two tag sets. They are all wired together through `viewModel` binding being the same variable. This is the result we get if we click on **Tails**:

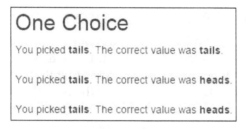

Well, it is the results we got that time. Actually, the results change pretty much every time we refresh the page. Now, we are ready to do something extra special by combining our AMD approach with Knockout modules.

Component-based SPAs

Now, we can look at one of the fastest growing trends in web development, the concept of single-page applications. The name is fancier than the practice because it is wrapped in confusion, but we will help you get over that here.

First, think of your website as a computer or mobile device. You can put multiple applications on your system. The apps can work together or independently. While we understand this for our computing systems, we seem to get confused when we move to web servers. Everything is not one application, or better put, rarely should everything be one application. There was a day, before Windows, when your spreadsheet and your word processor were shipped as one application. This was very popular, but over time we figured out packaging two apps was smarter than trying to build cross functionality into one app. Thus, we created office suites.

Today, we are suffering from the effects of mistakes made on most server platforms. When our backend server languages were created, many of them created a packaging approach that was wrapped around the term "application". So, when you built a website with a shopping cart, forum, and blog, they all ran under the same application scope. In hindsight, we should have labeled these site scopes and sub-divided the shopping "application", the forum "application", and the blog "application" as items under the "site".

Single-page applications seem to be having the same folly. The architecture and naming conventions tend to cause confusion. As a fellow seasoned developer, let me be vain for a moment and give you my permission to think outside the box on this. Forget the name SPA for a moment and let's step back and just understand what it does. Once you understand what it does, you will be able to smartly figure out how to apply it. Good implementation is after all, or it should be, the goal.

Best development strategies

There are many goals connected to the best development strategies. The truth is that there is no single best strategy. It is similar to the truth commonly shared as an answer in tech circles: it depends. This means the first thing you need to know is the target needs before you figure out what fits the best. Some people get caught up thinking bleeding-edge solutions are the best strategies. Sometimes they are, but not universally. It should be a heads-up, wide awake decision. The truth is that unless we are getting business done, technology doesn't add anything to the picture.

Technology is powerful. Technology is about knowing. If we properly understand the challenges then we can better choose our technology, our methodologies, and our solutions. Sometimes we may choose Knockout and other times just stay with jQuery. Sometimes, we bring in other mixes of products such as RequireJS and more.

Getting real

Another thing we should avoid is trying to apply technology we have never actually used anywhere. This is a high-stakes gamble, and this is why I hope you have been doing the code examples as you go through this book.

We are now going to create a solution, by popular name, an SPA, using Knockout and its components to drive the views. Because the concept is called SPA, we will call these dynamically loaded views "pages". We will be building on the AMD concept of dynamically loaded content using a few other SPA concepts as well. The goal here is not to teach you all the ins and outs of SPAs, but this will give you a pretty good launching point if you have never jumped in before.

Our page content, code if you prefer, will be sectioned off into a pages directory with each page having its template and `viewModel` in separate files. Earlier, we repeated the template and the ViewModel for on-page components. This time, we will be using components for on-page content as well as for declaring the main view content using components. For clarity, we have created a `components` folder for the non-page components; for instance, the navigation bar will be put in the `components` folder.

What makes an SPA fit for the basic description of a single page is that the browser only loads a base page at a time. After that, all content is pulled and injected into the page. So it is technically correct that there be only one page. The display of content on the page is loaded and updated on the fly, but technically speaking, it is still on the original page. This will be our `index.html` file. If you look in your exercise root folder, you will see a subdirectory called `spa` and another called `myspa`.

If you want to see a completed SPA, you can peek ahead and look at the SPA version. My suggestion is to build it up and take the discovery route. Only then compare it to the SPA version if you feel like you made a mistake. Here is a screenshot of our starting point with our `myspa` example:

> Home
>
> This is dynamic content presented on the home page.

This looks rather plain, but it is actually more complex than you would think. Power tools often look unimpressive while sitting on the shelf. It is worth looking at the code of the home page. Here is the View or the template file for the page:

```
<h2>Home</h2>
<p data-bind=: message'"html"></p>
```

Normally, when we look in Knockout for the binding data, we are looking for the base `viewModel` data. In this case, we are looking at the data contained in the `viewModel` component. Let's look at the code of the component and see where it comes from by looking for our message variable:

```
define(["knockout", "text!./view.html"], function(ko,
  homeTemplate) {
  function myViewModel(route) {
    this.message = ko.observable('This is dynamic content
  presented on the home page.');
  console.log(vmSPA);
  }
  return { viewModel: myViewModel, template: homeTemplate };
});
```

We see the `define` method here again, which tells us we are taking care of dependencies properly using RequireJS. We see in the `myViewModel` section of code the `viewModel` attribute message. Remember to use the `this` type scope or the attributes will not be properly bound and visible on `viewModel`.

We are just getting exposed to the tools of SPA sites and pages. While it may not be amazing yet, the beauty will present itself as you learn to use the tools here. It's like looking at the paint brushes of great artists. You would not have been able to predict the amazing paintings that came from them. It's time to teach you how to use the tools that create powerful SPA solutions and improve your mastery over web development.

Coding time

The first thing we will look at is our single page where everything is presented. Here is the code for the super-duper everything page:

```
<!DOCTYPE html>
<html lang="en">
<head>
  <meta charset="utf-8">
  <meta http-equiv="X-UA-Compatible" content="IE=edge">
  <title>SPA Guide</title>
  <link href="/share/css/bootstrap.min.css" rel="stylesheet">
  <link href="css/styles.css" rel="stylesheet">
  <script src="app/require.config.js"></script>
  <script data-main="app/startup" src="/share/js/require.js"></script>
</head>
<body>
  <div id="page" class="container" data-bind="component: { name:
  route().page, params: route }"></div>
</body>
</html>
```

We see two JavaScript files here. The first is a configuration file and the second is the RequireJS file. That is not all the JavaScript requires, but the RequireJS file will manage pulling in the core libraries needed for this site to run properly. This is contained in the configuration file. Let's take a look at that file:

```
// require.js looks for the following global when initializing
var require = {
    baseUrl: ".",
    paths: {
        "bootstrap":            "/share/js/bootstrap.min",
        "crossroads":           "/share/js/crossroads.min",
```

```
            "hasher":                    "/share/js/hasher.min",
            "jquery":                    "/share/js/jquery.min",
            "knockout":                  "/share/js/knockout",
            "knockout-projections":     "/share/js/knockout-projections.min",
            "signals":                   "/share/js/signals.min",
            "text":                      "/share/js/text"
        },
        shim: {
            "bootstrap": { deps: ["jquery"] }
        }
    };
```

This is the same kind of logic we used in our AMD example previously. You will notice that we are using several libraries in our code here. RequireJS handles much of the loading on demand, or as needed, if you prefer to state it that way.

You will also notice that in the body section of the `index.html` page there is a Knockout bound `div` element like this:

```
<div id="page" class="container" data-bind="component: { name:
    route().page, params: route }"></div>
```

This is how we pull the page content and drive it to the View for the user. If you are new to this kind of app, there is something that will appear to be missing. There is another file that is actually being called that is not immediately apparent. Look at the `script` tag that calls `require.js` into the page:

```
<script data-main="app/startup" src="/share/js/require.js"></script>
```

Notice the `data-main` attribute binding. This tells the page to load in the `starup.js` file from the `app` folder. Let's look at that file here:

```
define(['jquery', 'knockout', './router', 'bootstrap', 'knockout-
    projections'], function($, ko, router) {
    // General Components (can be packaged as AMD modules):
    // dynamic page components
    ko.components.register('home-page', { require: 'page/home/home'
    });
    // static page components
    // Start the application
    vmSPA = function() {
        this.route = router.currentRoute;
    };
    vm = new vmSPA();
    ko.applyBindings(vm);});
```

We see the `RequireJS` `define` method, and there is no return needed as the functionality here is to make sure things are bound right with Knockout. You will also see that it is declaring all the libraries it needs upfront, based on the array list with the settings in our `require.config.js` file.

The next thing you will see is the dynamic page components being registered. We only have one page at this time, so if you look in the `page/home` folder, you will see `home.js` and `view.html` as the files located there. We will look at those shortly, but they are the `viewModel` and `template` items for our page component.

Another aspect common to most SPAs is routing. The other JavaScript libraries handle this, and that is what is being bound to our global binding via the `route` attribute. All of this working together called that "less-than-awesome" page in the previous screenshot. The `router` file is the last piece of core pieces we need to work with as we build out, expanding our SPA. Let's look at its code:

```
define(["knockout", "crossroads", "hasher"], function(ko,
  crossroads, hasher) {

  return new Router({
    routes: [
      { url: '', params: { page: 'home-page' } }
    ]
  });
  function Router(config) {
    var currentRoute = this.currentRoute = ko.observable({});
    ko.utils.arrayForEach(config.routes, function(route) {
      crossroads.addRoute(route.url, function(requestParams) {
      currentRoute(ko.utils.extend(requestParams, route.params));
    });
  });
  activateCrossroads();
  }
  function activateCrossroads() {
          function parseHash(newHash, oldHash) {
                crossroads.parse(newHash);
          }
    crossroads.normalizeFn = crossroads.NORM_AS_OBJECT;
    hasher.initialized.add(parseHash);
    hasher.changed.add(parseHash);
    hasher.init();
  }
});
```

Again, we see the `define` method in action here, keeping dependencies properly managed. There is also the routing which includes routes, or will include routes. At this time, there is only one route, and that is to our home page view. This is where we will be handling more page views. The rest of the code here is needed for the routes to function, but you don't have to understand it any more than you have to understand jQuery core code to use jQuery. So, if you want to explore it, you are welcome to do so. Otherwise, just focus on what you need to know, which is the routes array segment of this code.

Adding navigation

We need to do two things to add the navigation. The component for navigation has already been created, so we are just adding it into our SPA solution. First, open the `startup.js` file in the `app` folder. Under the general components comment, add this line of code:

```
ko.components.register('nav-bar', { require: 'components/nav-bar/nav-bar' });
```

We need to register components before they are called, and this is where we are doing that in our SPA. Now, we will be able to add the `nav-bar` tag to the top of the `body` section of our body on the `index.html` file as follows:

```
<nav-bar params="route: route"></nav-bar>
```

Oh, while that does cover code, there is one more thing needed. To show our navigation, we need to take the content and the page view, and move it down enough to show the navigation. We put an ID of the page onto the element; so, open the `css/style.css` file and enter this code there:

```
#page {
  margin-top: 80px;
}
```

Go ahead and save and close that file as we will not need it again in this exercise. We now have a basic navigation bar for our SPA. This is how things look now:

Adding pages

Let's add an **About** page next. The **About** page will be different from our **Home** page because it will only contain static content. We will not be binding to viewModel this time. In the startup.js file, under the static page components comment, add this code:

```
ko.components.register('about-page', {
  template: { require: 'text!page/about/about.html' }
});
```

Notice we are only adding in a template, with no viewModel. We also need to add the link to our navigation. The code here is based on the use of Bootstrap. This is the code we would add after the home link in the code in the components/nav-bar/ nav-bar.html file:

```
<li data-bind="css: { active: route().page === 'about-page' }">
<a href="#about">About</a>
</li>
```

I like how easy it is to manage the active setting based on whether this route matches this page. If you look at the component we registered and the route().page comparison, you will see that the values will make the page active when they match. There is one more thing we will need to have our about page work—the about page component itself. In the page folder, copy the _base file as about.

The last thing to do to create a new page is to add the page to our Router array, which is in the app/router.js file:

```
{ url: 'about',      params: { page: 'about-page' } }
```

This is what our page looks like when we select the about navigation item. (If you are having problems getting it to show, reload the application to make it work once changes have been made.)

Notice the highlighting works wonderfully, giving the user feedback to validate the page they are actually viewing. The static content on this page and the dynamic content on the home page give us the foundation to understand how to build SPA sites. Yet, we can do better than that. We are going to add in a page that will allow us to update the Bootstrap skin that we are using to view the site.

Time for some custom style

We will start off by listing the things we do when we are adding another page to this form of Knockout-based SPA site:

1. Add a page component registration to the `startup.js` file in the `app` folder.
2. Add a menu item in the `nav-bar` tag if desired.
3. Add the router configuration to the `router.js` file in the `app` folder.
4. Create a new page in the `page` folder with appropriate files for `viewModel` and `template` code.

Here is the code for the first three steps. First is the registration code for the `startup.js` file. Add this right after the `home-page` component registration, as follows:

```
ko.components.register('bootstrap-page', { require:
  'page/bootstrap/bootstrap' });
```

Then we will add the following code to the `nav-bar` component:

```
<li data-bind="css: { active: route().page === 'bootstrap-page'
  }">
<a href="#bootstrap">Bootstrap</a>
</li>
```

Next, we will add the following code to that `router.js` file so our system knows how to handle the new routed item.

```
{ url: 'bootstrap', params: { page: 'bootstrap-page' } },
```

The final phase, of course, will be creating the actual page component files. Again, we will copy the _base folder. This time, rename the copy as `boostrap`. Inside the folder, rename the `_base.js` file as `bootstrap.js` and you will be ready to code. Here is the `template` code to get started. Place this code in the `view.html` file under the `page/bootstrap` folder as follows:

```
<h2>Bootstrap</h2>
<p data-bind='html: message'></p>
```

This will be our `viewModel` code to place in the `boostrap.js` file under the `page/bootstrap` folder:

```
define(["knockout", "text!./view.html"], function(ko,
  bootstrapTemplate) {
  function myViewModel(route) {
    this.message = ko.observable('Welcome to Bootstrap Page.');
  }
```

```
      return { viewModel: myViewModel, template: bootstrapTemplate };
   });
```

Now, when we run this code, here is the view we get after clicking on the **Bootstrap** nav menu. Ah, wait! Before saving the screenshot, it appeared to me that the header of the template was not visible. My CSS had not been saved, so the offset was not working right. Now, with the correction made, here is the correct view. You should find that the other views will also show correctly now. How many of you caught that looking at my screenshots? Here again, we will show the screenshot:

That certainly looks better. It is also starting to shape up and offer a promising site. We need to go in and modify our ViewModel to make this page highly functional. Before we do that, we need to actually go back to the main `index.html` file and add an `id` attribute to the page style tag as follows:

```
<link id="page_style" href="/share/css/bootstrap.min.css"
   rel="stylesheet">
```

This will allow us to use jQuery to target and update the page style for the page. Yes, we are using jQuery here and not Knockout. It still happens. Now, in the `bootstrap.js` file, replace the message variable with the following code:

```
var self = this;
self.message = ko.observable('Hello from the bootstrap component! \
On this page we will be letting you choose from different <a target="_
blank" href="http://bootswatch.com/">Bootswatch</a> themes.');
  self.theme = ko.observable('none');
  self.themes = ko.observableArray([]);
  self.themesVisible = ko.observable(true);
```

> Notice that we have used a slash as a line break to continue coding on the next line. Some of us are familiar with that shortcut, but others may appreciate the tip if they are not.

We then add the `theme`, `themes`, and `themesVisible` attributes to our ViewModel. We will also need a couple of methods added to the page. These will be the `loadThemes` and `changeTheme` methods.

The `loadThemes` method will be pulling a JSON-based data file, AJAX style. Again, we will be using jQuery for this functionality. Here is the content of the JSON file. I would suggest just copying the file over from the matching SPA if you are not a perfect typist. This will also go into the `page/bootstrap` folder:

```
{
    "theme": [
        { "name": "cerulean", "bg":"light"},
        { "name": "cosmo", "bg":"light"},
        { "name": "cyborg", "bg":"dark"},
        { "name": "darkly", "bg":"dark"},
        { "name": "flatly", "bg":"light"},
        { "name": "journal", "bg":"light"},
        { "name": "lumen", "bg":"light"},
        { "name": "paper", "bg":"light"},
        { "name": "readable", "bg":"light"},
        { "name": "sandstone", "bg":"light"},
        { "name": "simplex", "bg":"light"},
        { "name": "slate", "bg":"dark"   },
        { "name": "spacelab", "bg":"light"},
        { "name": "superhero", "bg":"dark"},
        { "name": "united", "bg":"light"},
        { "name": "yeti", "bg":"light" }
    ]
}
```

Now, we need to add the rest of the code to the `bootstrap.js` file in the `page/bootstrap` folder. First, we will add the `loadThemes` method. Here is the code for that:

```
myViewModel.prototype.loadThemes = function() {
    jQuery.getJSON("page/bootstrap/data.json")
    .done(function(data){
        self.themes(data.theme);
        self.themesVisible(false);
    }).fail(function(data){
        alert('fail data pull for Bootstrap page');
    });
};
```

This code will pull the data and push the data right into the data-bound themes array. Notice that we also included some code to show a very basic concept of exception handling. Now, add the code for the `changeTheme` function:

```
myViewModel.prototype.changeTheme = function(data,event) {
    var style =
    '/share/css/bootswatch/'+data.name+'/bootstrap.min.css';
    jQuery('#page_style').attr('href',style);
    vm.bg(data.bg);
};
```

We will be able to bind these methods in `viewModel` to handle event triggers in our template code. There is one extra thing though that we need to handle this functionality. Notice `vm.bg(data.bg)` at the end of that method. We are setting the value of the incoming item to set a global variable. It tells the system whether the background we are using is a light or dark background. We won't be using that yet, but we are creating it now to be used shortly. In order to do that, we need to add the following bit of code to our main site `starup.js` file in the `app` folder:

```
vmSPA = function(){
    this.route = router.currentRoute;
    this.bg = ko.obervable("light");
};
```

Now we can add our template code to the `view.html` file below the existing code. Notice that the button visibility is managed to improve user experience. When our data is loaded, we make the button invisible. We are also wiring the click method of the images to the `changeTheme` method on our `viewModel` component. At this time, there is no base variable alias for the component base, so we will use the `$parent` alias to target the method on the parent level of this data structure. Take a look at the following code:

```
<button data-bind="click: loadThemes, visible:
    themesVisible'">Load Themes</button>
<div class="row" data-bind="foreach: themes">
<div class="col-xs-6 col-md-3" style="text-align: center;">
    <img class="img-responsive img-thumbnail" data-bind="attr:{
    'src':'/share/css/bootswatch/'+$data.name+'/thumbnail.png'},
    click: $parent.changeTheme"></img>
    <br/><br/>
</div>
</div>
```

Okay, we are all wired up now. If you have issues, compare the code to the code in the SPA folder as that is working and is from where the example code for this rebuild practice exercise came. Here is the initial screenshot when reloading and selecting the Bootstrap navigation item:

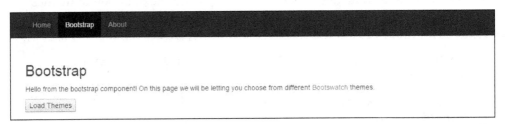

Oh, if you do not recognize them, these skin styles are open source styles offered by `bootswatch.com` for us to use. They also have commercial solutions there.

Now, we will click on the button to load our themes from the JSON-based data. This also could have been a live dynamic server location URL. This is what we get after clicking on the button:

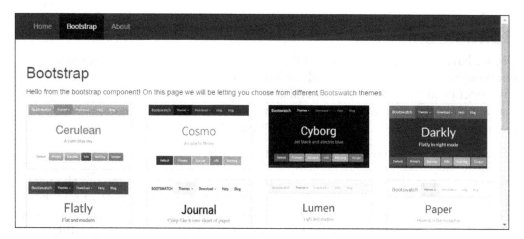

If we scroll down and click on **Superhero** and move our mouse, this is what we will see:

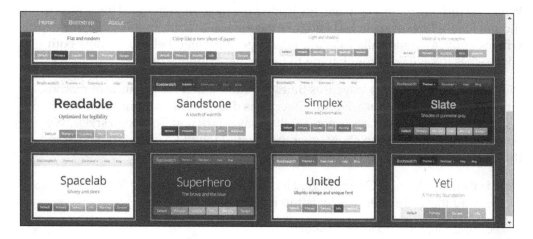

 I'm not sure why we have to move the mouse, but that will work most of the time; we would figure out an instant update if it was a live website, of course.

Now we are able to update the styles by choice on demand. If you move to different pages, you will see that the look stays. If this were a live login site, we would use AJAX to store the user style choices back on the server. We could also choose to store them in cookie variables, but then if the user goes to another machine, their choices will not travel with them. This is why we suggest you store them on a server when possible.

Bonus item

Oh, we have a bonus for this part of the book. This book is based on Knockout 3.2, but there is a nice change proposed for Knockout 3.3 that will let us address the component code with a component alias. It is very simple to update our code to try that out. First, we need to go to the `require.config.js` file in the `app` folder and make one change. We have to change the file the Knockout alias is targeting like so:

```
"knockout": "/share/js/knockout.3_3_alpha:
```

Then, we jump back into our `view.html` file in the `bootstrap` folder and change the `$parent` variable to `$component`. Next, we run our code again, which should work fine. This is more practical code, and if the data structure in a component were more complex, this pragmatic alias would just keep the code as simple as it should.

Building cross-page interaction

When we did our Bootstrap page, we loaded the data on demand. This means it did not load till the user clicked and told the themes to load. In this page, the data will instantly, automatically load onto the page. It seemed helpful to show both approaches to save you from having to figure these options out.

We will be using a jQuery page this time. We choose that for a couple of reasons. Firstly, we happen to appreciate all jQuery has done for the community over the years. The second reason is we noticed they have dark and light logo styles. We borrowed their graphics to show what they would look like on a dark Boostrap theme as well as on a light Bootstrap theme.

Here is the code for our jQuery page. First is the registration code for the `startup.js` file. Add this code after the Bootstrap registration:

```
ko.components.register('jquery-page',
{ require: 'page/jquery/jquery' });
```

Then we will add the following code to the `nav-bar` component:

```
<li data-bind="css: { active: route().page === 'jquery-page' }">
  <a href="#jquery">jQuery</a>
</li>
```

Next, we will add this code to the `router.js` file so our system knows how to handle the new routed item. This is the full router section of code at this point:

```
return new Router({
  routes: [
    { url: '',          params: {page: 'home-page' } },
    { url: 'about',     params: {page: 'about-page' } },
    { url: 'bootstrap', params: {page: 'bootstrap-page' } },
    { url: 'jquery',     params:{ page: 'jquery-page' } }
  ]
});
```

The final phase, of course, will be creating the actual page component files. Again, we will copy the _base folder. This time, rename the copy as `jquery`. Inside the folder, rename the `_base.js` file as `jquery.js` and you will be ready to code. We also have files to pull over from the working version of this SPA. We will be pulling the `data.json` file and the `logos` folder.

We can now edit our `viewmodel` file first. Here is the code for the `jquery.js` file:

```
define(['knockout', 'text!./view.html'], function(ko,
  templateMarkup) {
  function myViewModel(params) {
    var self = this;
    self.message = ko.observable('Hello from the jQuery
component!');
    self.project = ko.observableArray();
jQuery.getJSON('page/jquery/data.json').done(function(data){
      self.project(data.project);
    }).fail(function(){
      alert("AJAX error on jQuery Page View.");
    });
  }
  myViewModel.prototype.logo = function(data,event) {
    var url = 'page/jquery/logos/'+data.base+'-mark-
'+vm.bg()+'.gif';
    return url;
  };
  // This runs when the component is torn down. Put here any logic
necessary to clean up,
  // for example cancelling setTimeouts or disposing Knockout
subscriptions/computeds.
  myViewModel.prototype.dispose = function() { };
  return { viewModel: myViewModel, template: templateMarkup };
});
```

We again have our `defined` method, which takes the values of the two items and passes them into the function as parameters. The declarations are straightforward with one difference. This time, we are passing the results of a `jQuery JSON` request into the `self.project` binding. We again have a very basic exception handling, in case there are exceptions, as they are part of awesome coding. This time, the method we are creating in this component is a method to set the logo name. Here is our `view.html` code so we can look at how it was integrated. Note that inside the method, we are again using the main SPA `viewModel` binding to pull the light or dark background:

```
<h2>jQuery</h2>
<p data-bind="text: message'"></p>
<div class="row" data-bind="foreach: project">
  <div class="col-md-4">
    <img class="img-responsive img-thumbnail" data-bind="attr:{
'src':$ component.logo($data)}">
  </div>
  <div class="col-md-8">
    <h3 data-bind="text:$ data.name"></h3>
    <span data-bind="html:$ data.description"></span>
  </div>
  <div class="clearfix"></div>
</div>
```

Here, we see our template will loop through each project that was returned from our AJAX call to the JSON data. Notice that we are using the `$component` item for the logo. If you are still not using Knockout 3.3 alpha code, or need to deploy with something else, you should change that back to `$parent` to make sure it works correctly without that enhancement. Otherwise, this is standard template code.

With this in place, here is what the jQuery page will look like with a fresh reload and selection of the jQuery navigation tab:

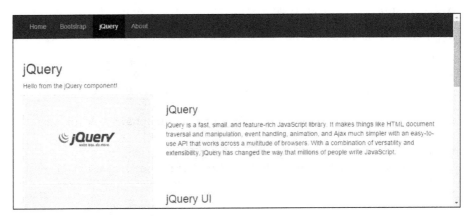

By default, the setting for the background is set to light and the logos it shows are the lighter logos. Now, we will jump to the Bootstrap page and select a darker style. This is what it will look like with the style we select:

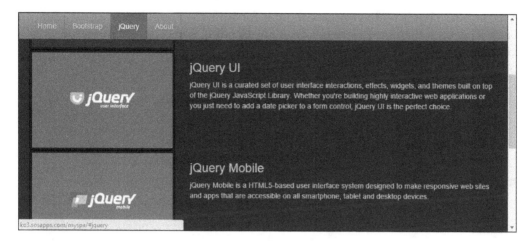

Now we have a very nice looking app to show off. While it may not do everything you have seen on any website, what it does will impress many a client or friend.

What next?

There are many plugins and ways to package and advance your abilities as a developer using Knockout. I will be opening up a resource at `http://knockout.developers.zone` where we will be sharing links and tips, and hope to have a meet-up or two over the next year for fellow Knockout developers.

Summary

This chapter has pulled together concepts from every chapter and shown the awesome power of templates working together with ViewModels within Knockout components. You should now have an awesome foundation to do more with less than ever before. You should know how to mingle your jQuery code with the Knockout code side by side.

To review, in this chapter, we learned what Knockout components are. We learned how to use the components to create custom HTML elements that are interactive and powerful. We learned how to enhance custom elements to allow variables to be managed using the more common attributes approach. We learned how to use an AMD-style approach to coding with Knockout. We also learned how to AJAX everything and integrate jQuery to enhance Knockout-based solutions.

Many people struggle to understand the concept of SPA or single-page application sites. We were able to create a single-page application that provides understanding and perspective. In fact, this could be the beginning of your next site.

What's next? That is up to you. One thing is for sure, the possibilities are broader using Knockout than they were before. Happy coding and congratulations on completing your study of KnockoutJS!

Index

A

Action Message Format (AMF) 78
AJAX
  KnockoutJS, connecting 82-85
array collections
  about 33-36
  last item, removing 37, 38
array collections, functions
  destroy() 34
  destroyAll() 34
  pop() 34
  push() 34
  remove() 34
  removeAll() 34
  reverse() 34
  shift() 34
  sort() 34
  splice() 34
  unshift() 34
arrays 31, 32
Asynchronous module
     definition (AMD) 127, 138-141
attribute handling
  enhancing 131-133

B

best development strategies, SPAs
  about 142
  applying 142, 143
bootstrap component example 136, 137
browser developer tools
  shortcuts 16
  using 13-15

bubbling
  about 57
  preventing 57

C

calculations
  automating 20-22
  final total calculation 25, 26
  subtotal calculation 22, 23
  tax time, calculating 23, 24
checkbox binding
  about 62-65
  enhanced event integration 66
  with visibility 54, 55
closure 20
collection handling
  with templates 107-111
components
  about 127-129
  dynamic component selection 130
  element 131
  template section 128
  viewModel section 128
computations
  purifying 95-97
computed context
  getDependenciesCount() function 100
  isInitial() function 99
  using 99, 100
computed observable
  creating, with Form 1 97
  creating, with Form 2 98
  creating, with Form 3 98

creating, with Form 4 99
dispose() function 99
extend(extenders) function 99
getDependenciesCount() function 99
getSubscriptionsCount() function 99
isActive() function 99
peek() function 99
subscribe(callback [,callbackTarget, event])
    function 99
using 99
conditional binding 29, 30
custom libraries
building 133-136
custom tags 131

D

data
sorting 38-41
unmapping 85-87
Document Object Model (DOM) 6
DOM elements
binding 7, 8
CSS, binding 10
HTML, binding 9
multi-binding 12, 13
numbers, binding 10, 11
text, binding 8, 9
visibility, managing 11, 12
Don't Repeat Yourself (DRY) 41
drawer 17

E

element 131
event binding
about 51, 52
bubbling, preventing 57
checkbox, binding with visibility 54, 55
default actions 56
markup, binding 52-54
modifier keys 55, 56
event handling
with templates 112-114

F

Firebug 13
Form 1, computed observable
evaluator 97
ko.computed(evaluator [, targetObject,
    options]) 97
options 97
targetObject 97
Form 2, computed observable
deferEvaluation 98
disposeWhen 98
disposeWhenNodeIsRemoved 98
owner 98
pure 98
read 98
write 98
Form 3, computed observable
ko.pureComputed(evaluator
    [, targetObject]) 98
Form 4, computed observable
ko.pureComputed(options) 99

G

Google Chrome
using 13
grid forms
creating 72-75
grid plugin
code, executing 42-46
data, sorting 47-49
working with 41, 42

H

Handlebars 114

I

installation, KnockoutJS 5, 6
internal functions
hidden features, preventing 20
using 18, 19

J

JSON
about 78
URL 78
ViewModel, converting 78-81

K

KnockoutJS
connecting, with AJAX 82-85
debugger 15, 16
installing 5, 6
templates 101
URL 6, 157
KnockoutJS context debugger
about 16
URL, for downloading 16
KOmponents
URL 132
ko.toJS method
using 78
ko.toJSON method
using 78
ko.utils.arrayFilter() function 88-90
ko.utils.arrayFirst() function 90, 91
ko.utils.arrayForEach() function 93, 94
ko.utils.arrayGetDistinctValues()
function 92, 93
ko.utils.arrayMap() function 91, 92
ko.utils.compareArrays() function 94, 95

L

list editor
creating, for list management 70-72

M

mail merge 101
mapped data
merging 87
mapping
about 81, 82
with options 88

markup
binding 52-54
Model 7
Model View ViewModel (MVVM) 6, 7

N

native templates 101-106
navigation, SPAs
adding 147
bonus item 154
cross page interaction, building 154-157
custom style 149-154
pages, adding 148
non-Knockout functions
working with 26

P

pureComputed method
versus computed method 95-97

R

radio button binding
about 62-65
enhanced event integration 65, 66
Ruby on Rails (RoR) 34

S

Safari
using 13
select binding
about 66-68
elements, selecting with object
collections 68, 69
list editor, creating for list
management 70-72
shortcuts, browser developer tools
about 16
AJAX, inspecting 17
device emulation 17
DOM, inspecting 17

resources, inspecting 17
URL 16
single page applications (SPAs)
about 141, 142
best development strategies 142
code 144-147
navigation, adding 147
sorting, data 38-41
subscribe method
using, in third-party template 117-121
subscriber 95

T

templates
about 101
native templates 101-106
options, exploring 121-124
used, for enhanced collection
handling 107-111
used, for event handling 112-114
textInput binding
about 57, 58
dynamic page, creating 58-62
third-party template
about 114
handling, with Underscore 114-116
modified template handling, with
Underscore 116, 117
subscribe method, using 117-121
updating 117-121

U

Underscore
about 114
modified template, handling 116, 117
used, for handling third-party
template 114-116
uniqueName binding 72
unmapping, data 85-87
user interface (UI) 45
utility functions
about 88
ko.utils.arrayFilter() 88-90
ko.utils.arrayFirst() 90, 91
ko.utils.arrayForEach() 93, 94
ko.utils.arrayGetDistinctValues() 92, 93
ko.utils.arrayMap() 91, 92
ko.utils.compareArrays() 94, 95

V

View 6
ViewModel
about 7
converting, to JSON 78-81

Thank you for buying
KnockoutJS Web Development

About Packt Publishing

Packt, pronounced 'packed', published its first book, *Mastering phpMyAdmin for Effective MySQL Management*, in April 2004, and subsequently continued to specialize in publishing highly focused books on specific technologies and solutions.

Our books and publications share the experiences of your fellow IT professionals in adapting and customizing today's systems, applications, and frameworks. Our solution-based books give you the knowledge and power to customize the software and technologies you're using to get the job done. Packt books are more specific and less general than the IT books you have seen in the past. Our unique business model allows us to bring you more focused information, giving you more of what you need to know, and less of what you don't.

Packt is a modern yet unique publishing company that focuses on producing quality, cutting-edge books for communities of developers, administrators, and newbies alike. For more information, please visit our website at www.packtpub.com.

About Packt Open Source

In 2010, Packt launched two new brands, Packt Open Source and Packt Enterprise, in order to continue its focus on specialization. This book is part of the Packt Open Source brand, home to books published on software built around open source licenses, and offering information to anybody from advanced developers to budding web designers. The Open Source brand also runs Packt's Open Source Royalty Scheme, by which Packt gives a royalty to each open source project about whose software a book is sold.

Writing for Packt

We welcome all inquiries from people who are interested in authoring. Book proposals should be sent to author@packtpub.com. If your book idea is still at an early stage and you would like to discuss it first before writing a formal book proposal, then please contact us; one of our commissioning editors will get in touch with you.

We're not just looking for published authors; if you have strong technical skills but no writing experience, our experienced editors can help you develop a writing career, or simply get some additional reward for your expertise.

[PACKT] PUBLISHING open source
community experience distilled

KnockoutJS Starter

ISBN: 978-1-78216-114-1   Paperback: 50 pages

Learn how to knock out your next app in no time with KnockoutJS

1. Learn something new in an Instant!
   A short, fast, focused guide delivering immediate results.

2. Learn how to develop a deployable app as the author walks you through each step.

3. Understand how to customize and extend KnockoutJS to take your app to the next level.

Real-time Web Application Development using Vert.x 2.0

ISBN: 978-1-78216-795-2   Paperback: 122 pages

An intuitive guide to building applications for the real-time web with the Vert.x platform

1. Get started with developing applications for the real-time web.

2. From concept to deployment, learn the full development workflow of a real-time web application.

3. Utilize the Java skills you already have while stepping up to the next level.

Please check **www.PacktPub.com** for information on our titles

Building UIs with Wijmo

ISBN: 978-1-84969-606-7   Paperback: 116 pages

Build user interfaces quickly using widgets

1. Learn to configure Wijmo components for common usage scenarios.

2. Build adaptive websites that work on desktops and mobile devices.

3. Integrate Wijmo with Knockout to develop real-time applications.

jQuery HOTSHOT

ISBN: 978-1-84951-910-6   Paperback: 296 pages

Ten practical projects that exercise your skill, build your confidence, and help you master jQuery

1. See how many of jQuery's methods and properties are used in real situations. Covers jQuery 1.9.

2. Learn to build jQuery from source files, write jQuery plugins, and use jQuery UI and jQuery Mobile.

3. Familiarise yourself with the latest related technologies like HTML5, CSS3, and frameworks like Knockout.js.

Please check **www.PacktPub.com** for information on our titles

www.ingramcontent.com/pod-product-compliance
Lightning Source LLC
Chambersburg PA
CBHW060135060326
40690CB00018B/3889